Freewheeling

Freewheeling

How to let go a little, love a lot and discover life in all its fullness

Authentic
MEDIA

MILTON KEYNES • COLORADO SPRINGS • HYDERABAD

Copyright © 2007 Ruth Adams and Jan Harney

13 12 11 10 09 08 07   7 6 5 4 3 2 1

First published 2007 by Authentic Media,
9 Holdom Avenue, Bletchley, Milton Keynes MK1 1QR, UK
1820 Jet Stream Drive, Colorado Springs, CO 80921, USA
OM Authentic Media, Medchal Road, Jeedimetla Village,
Secunderabad 500 055, A.P., India www.authenticmedia.co.uk

Authentic Media is a division of IBS-STL U.K., limited by guarantee,
with its Registered Office at Kingstown Broadway, Carlisle, Cumbria CA3 0HA.
Registered in England & Wales No. 1216232. Registered charity 270162

British Library Cataloguing in Publication Data
A catalogue record for this book is available from the British Library.

Scripture quotations taken from the HOLY BIBLE NEW INTERNATIONAL
VERSION ®, NIV ® Copyright © 1973, 1978, 1984 by International Bible
Society ®. Used by permission. All rights reserved worldwide.'; Holy Bible New
Living translation, copyright © 1966, 2004. Used by permission of Tyndale
House Publishers, Inc., Wheaton, Illinois 60189. All rights reserved; and
The Message. Copyright © 1993, 1994, 1995, 1996, 2000, 2001, 2002.
Used by permission of NavPress Publishing Group.

ISBN: 978-1-85078-752-5

Cover Design and Typesetting by Adam Lees
Print Management by Adare
Printed in Great Britain by J.H. Haynes & Co., Sparkford

Contents

THERE MUST BE MORE
TO LIFE THAN THIS!

There must be more to life than this!

If you've ever said it or even thought it, then this book is for you.

Ask yourself the question 'If I won the lottery or found I only had six months to live, would I still be doing this?' That might sound like a sweeping generalisation, but it's a good way of assessing whether or not you are completely content with every aspect of your life.

One in five interviewees longed for more friends, with 18-30 year-olds outnumbering pensioners by far in feeling isolated. The search for jobs means that this generation is mobile and going off to university often cuts teenagers off from their school friends – yet around 22 per cent wished they were better educated and a quarter of us would like to find a more fulfilling job.

'I'M INTERESTED IN THE FUTURE Charles Kettering
BECAUSE I'M GOING TO SPEND THE REST OF MY LIFE THERE.'

The Readers Digest ran a nationwide poll recently to discover what people would change about their lives, given the chance. Unsurprisingly 77 per cent wanted to be wealthier. Although only about 7 per cent wished they were more religious, around a third of people interviewed wished they could bring someone back from the dead – usually because they left something unsaid or they were lonely.

Inevitably, around a third of people wished they were more attractive and there were many people who felt that their sex lives could be better, yet only 7 per cent regretted their choice of marriage partner and (happily) none of the people interviewed were dissatisfied with having children or wished to change gender, race or their parents.

Yet, all in all, a whopping 97 per cent would change something about their lives, given the chance.

Clearly there are some things that can't be changed because of current circumstances, but many can and we've discovered that when we are able to improve other areas of our lives, then our perspective and attitude to the static things is much more positive.

We're conscious that no-one can prescribe a perfect lifestyle for someone else – we're all unique beings with different personalities and preferences. So this book is not meant to provide off-the-peg answers to complex situations. We've chosen instead to pose some questions and offer some tools for exploration that we've found helpful.

Nor do we profess to know all the answers. We believe that life is a journey and this book is part of our own voyage of discovery. Like you, we're continuing to explore, research, experience and question. Why not journey with us?

'HAPPINESS IS A JOURNEY, NOT A DESTINATION.'
Father Alfred D'Souza

You can simply work through the eight chapters by yourself. Alternatively, you might go through it with your partner or a close friend. Or you might like to consider getting together a group of friends and booking eight sessions in your diary to meet.

If you opt for the latter, we recommend that you each read the section before meeting and then go through it together, using the Talkback session at the end to summarise.

We've deliberately left some blank pages for you to write your own notes and observations and we offer our thoughts and findings along the way, conscious that this is only the beginning of a life-long quest.

We hope you enjoy the ride. Ruth & Jan

LIFE SHOULD NOT BE A
GRAVE WITH THE INTENT
IN AN ATTRACTIVE AND
BUT RATHER TO SKID IN
IN ONE HAND – STRAWBE
BODY THOROUGHLY USED
AND SCREAMING 'WOO...

JOURNEY TO THE
ION OF ARRIVING SAFELY
WELL PRESERVED BODY,
SIDEWAYS, CHAMPAGNE
RRIES IN THE OTHER,
UP, TOTALLY WORN OUT
WOO... WHAT A RIDE.'

AUTHOR UNKNOWN

How are you doing so far?

In many life coaching circles, the wheel of life is used to help identify those areas which need particular attention and we found ourselves asking 'Why circles?' Maybe it's because the earth is round, yet so often we live our lives with a linear attitude.

Example graph...

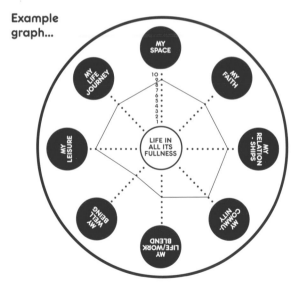

So much of what is important to us is measured in horizontals and verticals – we talk about the top and bottom lines – yet life is composed of seasons and cycles, spirals rather than verticals.

Take a look at our example graph on the left, now try filling your own scores in the blank graph on page 80 (centre-fold).

Begin by putting a mark on each line, indicating your satisfaction level with each segment. An ideal life would score a 10 on the outside edge for each and provide the perfect circle. However, for most of us, there will be 2s, 5s and 7s included in our scores, giving a slightly odd shaped 'circle'.

Take a few minutes now to score yourself on each of these areas. You might find that your relationships are going well right now and give yourself an '8' here, while for health you may only score a '2'.

There are no right or wrong answers. Priorities are different for each one of us depending on circumstances, life choices and what we ultimately consider to be important. Some of us will score highly in some areas and lower in others and this might prove helpful in indicating some of the issues that need looking at first.

You'll notice that our circle has 'Life in all its fullness' in the centre. We think that in life there should be space to work, rest and play; to read and think, listen and discuss, create something wonderful, laugh, cry and sing.

We've taken each of these sections as a separate chapter and approached it in a variety of ways that we hope will resonate with some aspect of your life. Each section is deliberately general, allowing you to be more specific about what you look at in each area. For example, in 'Personal Growth' you might have been planning to go to the gym regularly or intending to take a new course or attempt something new, but somehow, with other areas taking priority, this hasn't happened. So a '3' here gives the potential to increase the score quite quickly by ensuring that the good intention becomes a reality.

You've probably heard the anecdote about the man who stopped in a strange town and asked directions, only to be told 'You can't get there from here!'

Sometimes life can be like that. We have dreams and aspirations but it can seem a complicated journey from where we are currently to where we want to be.

We hope you'll find this book helpful in moving forward. More important still is that you find it to be informative, refreshing, inspirational and fun.

'THE UNIVERSE IS AN IMMEASURABLE WHEEL, TURNING FOREVER MORE...

REVEALING WITH EACH PASS, THINGS UNSEEN BEFORE.'

Longfellow

ONE DAY SHERLOCK HOLMES AND

AS THE NIGHT WORE ON, SHERLOC
AND ASKED WATSON 'WHAT DO YOU

WATSON RESPONDED 'I SEE THE NC
US TO THIS SPOT. BEYOND THAT I S
OF ORION. I CAN ALSO MAKE OUT
AND KNOW THAT THERE ARE UNIV

WATSON WAS ABOUT TO CONTINU
WHEN SHERLOCK ELBOWED HIM A
SOMEONE HAS STOLEN OUR TENT

There are two viewpoints here. One is that Watson was concentrating on the beauty he saw around him, focus
possible. The other is that Watson had simply missed the obvious. Which do you think it was?

WATSON WENT CAMPING.

WOKE UP, LEANED OVER

EE?'

RTH STAR WHICH HAS GUIDED

E THE BIG DIPPER AND THE TAIL

HE EDGES OF THE MILKY WAY

RSES EXPANDING BEYOND THAT.'

HIS RAPTUROUS EXPLANATION

D HISSED, 'WATSON, YOU IDIOT,

the positives, while Sherlock Holmes was more concerned about the crime, which made their new view

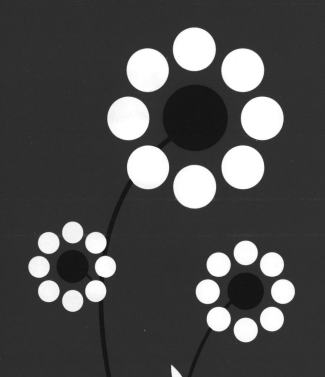

MY LIFE JOURNEY

Personal growth

If you were to write down now 'Who you are', how would you define yourself? Take a minute to write your immediate thoughts below.

Q Was what you wrote linked to your job?

Q Marital status?

Q Your children, if you have any?

Have you done one of the various personality profiling exercises that are available now? You can discover online whether you're an introvert or an extrovert – as if you didn't already know. In the cause of research, we've both been analysed in every which way – with varying levels of satisfaction and usefulness.

Most personality profiles are based on four main personality types but will describe them in different ways. For example, we now know that we're a Lion and an Otter, that we're Choleric and Sanguine (which we think sound like medieval diseases) and that we consist of four letters which neither of us can ever remember and that we're reasonably good at expressing our wants and needs.

Oh yes and we're a flibbertigibbet and a bossy moo respectively but we're not going to tell you who is what! None of this was particularly helpful in our opinion and although we recognise that people have found some of the other profile tools useful, we were about to cut our losses and give up the research.

And then we discovered PEP™.

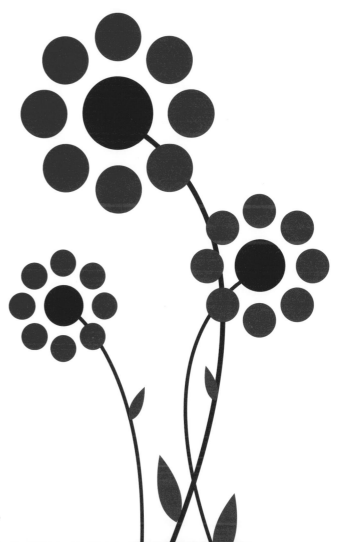

Most of us describe ourselves in terms of our job description, 'I am a teacher', 'a salesperson' or 'a social worker' or in terms of our various roles 'I am a mother', 'a wife', 'a friend.' None of these describe accurately or capture who we really are.

Different personality types value different things and our values determine our actions and our actions determine our results. Different values lead to strength – and conflict in any relationships, from families to the work place.

Part of making the right decisions that work for you is in knowing yourself well and this can help in making informed choices about career, family and relationships that help you to be the best you can be. A personality profile can help in this.

There are many personality profile assessments available. But how many of us, having spent time and money trying to find out 'who we are', are unable to recall our rating or characteristics within a short time of having completed the assessment?

But we found PEP™ (The Path Elements Profile) was different and we're both hooked on it; so much so that, on a whim, we took a plane to LA a while ago and were trained in this profile. It has transformed our lives.

The profile comes from a book by Laurie Beth Jones called The Four Elements of Success,[1] based on the four elements of wind, water, fire and water. It's an easily remembered profile and the team we both work with in Activate has developed a whole new language, as we understand each other so much better now that we've all done our profiles.

We all found it helped free us up to be who we really are. Once we understood our elements, we found we could accept ourselves and work to our strengths rather than try and be what other people wanted us to be. PEP™ could revolutionise your life, your family and your workplace as you begin to understand both yourself and others better.

What makes PEP™ so effective is that it is short, simple, sound, sticky and spreadable. Using the highly visual and universally understood elements of earth, water, wind and fire, the PEP™ taps into what people already know at some level about themselves and provides new layers of understanding about who they are and what makes them tick.

It can be taught quickly, applied immediately and become part of your family or team culture within minutes. It is infectious and healing in its applications. In our families, the elements have now become part of the normal conversation and the ability to produce a matrix of any two people or team means that it extends beyond one person and can be used for couples, pre-marriage courses, in education or the workplace.

We know we're all different, yet often fail to understand the way each personality thinks.

For example, Earths crave order and structure, Water personalities thrive with harmony and calm, Winds love flexibility while Fires thrive in atmospheres of challenge.

Jan is a (high!) wind/fire and Ruth a fire/wind. We're trying to ensure that the language in this book is as inclusive as we can make it – so that those of you with the earth and water elements feel you can relate to what's being said.

More details about this profile is available at www.in-your-element.co.uk

Goals

Think about the following questions. Or even better, get together with a friend and discuss them together:

Q What are your goals for the next year?

Our minds tend to go blank when faced with a question like this and if this is what happens to you too, then take a look at www.43things.com – a website which encourages visitors to check out the goals of thousands of other people around the world and find inspiration by reading the aspirations of others.

Q What three things would you most like to change about your life now?

Don't get bogged down with whether these things are possible, just write them down. How much would your life alter if these things were different?

Q Lots of individuals and organisations now have a mission statement. Ours is: To experience and inspire life in all its fullness. Have you ever considered writing a personal mission statement for your life? What would it be?

'GOALS ARE DREAMS WITH A DEADLINE.'

Brian Tracy

This isn't something you can do without plenty of thought but it might be an idea to begin considering now. Laurie Beth Jones' book The Path2 (Hyperion books, New York, 1996) is worth reading to help you think about this in more detail.

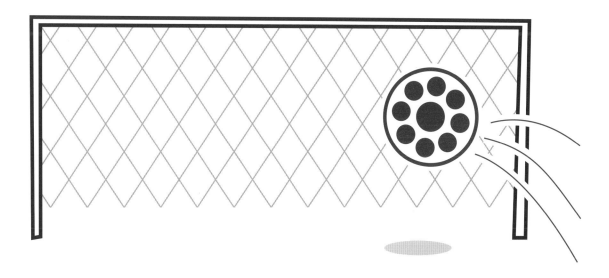

Life Coaching

Some of us find that a network of friends we can chat regularly to about life, love and the issues that bother us is essential. Ruth and a friend, who rarely see each other as they live at opposite ends of the country, email each other almost daily and both find this relationship of mutual support and offloading incredibly helpful. Sometimes it's in looking outwards that we find the answers to our own problems.

Q Do you have friends that you can be real with, no matter what issues you're facing? Remind yourself of who they are.

For others, prayer provides the opportunity to take time out while they talk to God about the things they don't feel they can share with anyone else; while some people find that a detached professional can provide the necessary support.

Life coaches are increasingly being seen as the answer for those looking for a new focus. The role of a life coach is to help you untangle the difficulties, plan the route with clarity and enjoy the ride as you work towards your goal. A life coach will help you to focus on your strengths and use them to best advantage. They will assist you to unlock your potential and make the most of opportunities.

If we look at the New Testament in the Bible, we see that Jesus was the Master Life Coach. People flocked to him. He constantly affirmed them, challenged and inspired them. His coming to earth was the greatest single act of rapport building in the world.

It's hard to read the Bible without realising that Jesus gave people a clear goal to aim for, a map and compass to travel by and a promise that he'd be alongside them. Good coaches do that. In fact, Jesus often comes up in secular life coaching contexts as a model to follow.

Take another look at the characteristics of a life coach.

Q Are there lessons for you in the way you relate to other people?

Q Which of the phrases help you see where you might be more effective with your friends, families and work colleagues?

While we can't all be life coaches, we can ensure we develop some of the qualities necessary to make us more approachable and take an honest look at our own lives and see what practical steps we can take to improve things. No-one can make changes for us, it's our own personal journey, but as you go through this book, we hope you will find some pointers to help you along the way.

The Jar and the Coffee

The following story illustrates well how important it is to define your priorities, so when things in life seem almost too much to handle, when 24 hours in a day are not enough, remember the mayonnaise jar and the two cups of coffee.

A professor stood before his philosophy class and had some items in front of him. When the class began, wordlessly, he picked up a very large and empty mayonnaise jar and proceeded to fill it with golf balls.

He then asked the students if the jar was full. They agreed that it was.

The professor then picked up a box of pebbles and poured them into the jar. He shook the jar lightly.

The pebbles rolled into the open areas between the golf balls. He then asked the students again if the jar was full. They agreed it was.

The professor next picked up a box of sand and poured it into the jar. Of course, the sand filled up everything else. He asked once more if the jar was full. The students responded with a unanimous 'Yes.'

The professor then produced two cups of coffee from under the table and poured the entire contents into the jar, effectively filling the empty space between the sand. The students laughed.

'Now,' said the professor, as the laughter subsided, 'I want you to recognize that this jar represents your life. The golf balls are the important things, your faith, your family, your children, your health, your friends and your favourite passions – things that if everything else was lost and only they remained, your life would still be full.'

'The pebbles are the other things that matter like your job, your house and your car. The sand is everything else, the small stuff.'

'If you put the sand into the jar first,' he continued, 'there is no room for the pebbles or the golf balls. The same goes for life. If you spend all your time and energy on the small stuff, you will never have room for the things that are important to you. Pay attention to the things that are critical to your happiness. Play with your children. Take time to get medical check-ups. Take your partner out to dinner. Play another 18.

There will always be time to clean house and fix the disposal. Take care of the golf balls first, the things that really matter. Set your priorities. The rest is just sand.'

One of the students raised her hand and inquired what the coffee represented. The professor smiled. 'I'm glad you asked. It just goes to show you that no matter how full your life may seem, there's always room for a couple of cups of coffee with a friend.'

Self Worth

Most of us are aware that improvements could be made to our image and self confidence with just a few simple changes.

It might mean regular visits to the hairdressers, a browse through one of Trinny and Susannah's books to give an idea of what clothes might suit us, or treating ourselves to a colour session to learn what shades will help us look our best.

None of these options need to cost lots of money and if we get together with a few friends and give each other the benefit of an honest appraisal, it could be great fun too. Colour me Beautiful and House of Colour have a list of consultants nationwide on their websites and they'll be happy to arrange a consultation and show how wearing the right colours for your skin tone can transform what you buy and how you look.

Jan had a session like this ten years ago and loved it so much that she took fourteen of her friends to the consultant to have a confidence boost. As she was treating many of them to the session, she was in danger of running up an overdraft equal to the national debt! Fortunately, the local college near Jan's home ran a twelve-week course in Colour Consultation and she was able to study this and qualify. As she doesn't have a franchise – she buys her colour drapes and shopping swatches independently – she isn't obliged to bring in a set level of business, so it suits her well. It suits Ruth too as she (and three of her daughters) were Jan's guinea pigs.

For many of us, although we can look great on the outside, we still suffer from a lack of self worth. This condition seems almost universal amongst our friends, most of who deal with it very wittily. As a result, we both get lots of emails with various pieces of advice, humour and sarcasm, which drop into our inbox on a daily basis.

Your self-esteem affects the whole of your life and it is something that you carry with you every minute of the day. When your self-esteem is healthy, you feel good and you can be much more positive about your life. When your self-esteem is low, it affects the way you view every area of your life. Imagine how you would feel if you had a such a positive self esteem that you felt confident and managed to cope with most things that life throws at you – and still had enough energy left to enjoy life to the full!

One of the most inspirational websites that we've found which deals with self esteem is www.selfesteem4women.com. You can go onto the website and take a free online self-esteem test which highlights the areas which might need some attention. We both found it a really helpful and revealing test when we did it. The website editors also offer some techniques to improve self esteem. You can even sign up for a free regular email covering issues that many of us struggle with.

Some life coaches advocate ending each day by making a list of ten good things you've achieved that day, or ten things you like about yourself. We think that would be a very good start towards developing self-worth. Why not give it a try?

Start today.

Q What would today's list look like?

1. _____
2. _____
3. _____
4. _____
5. _____
6. _____
7. _____
8. _____
9. _____
10. _____

Some people may find they struggle to find ten positive things to say, while others could list lots more. If you struggled, then a course on self worth might be a start in helping you to be more realistic about yourself.

Family Caring have a downloadable self worth course for adults on their website – www.familycaring.co.uk/Self-esteem. It might be helpful to go through this with a few friends, allowing about two hours to complete it.

It's only an introduction to the whole subject of self worth and it may bring things to light which can be worked on more fully in the future with a close friend or counsellor. What comes to light can be used towards personal growth and wholeness.

Our perception of who we really are, deep down, will affect every other part of our lives, including our relationships and our happiness levels. There's a danger that we can work so hard on the outside, on how we look and what we wear, that we neglect who we are inside. We both have this sense that we're of great worth because of who God made us to be.

One of our favourite passages in the Bible is in Psalm 139, which says,

Oh yes, you shaped me first inside, then out: you formed me in my mother's womb... Body and soul, I am marvellously made! I worship in adoration – what a creation! You know me inside and out, you know every bone in my body; You know exactly how I was made, bit by bit, how I was sculpted from nothing into something. Like an open book, you watched me grow from conception to birth; all the stages of my life were spread out before you, The days of my life all prepared before I'd even lived one day.

(*The Message*: Psalm139:13-16)

Words like that make us feel special – but we do recognise that some people have had such difficult experiences in their past that their self worth is very low and words are simply not enough. Specialist help might be needed to help them see themselves in a positive light. There are some excellent counsellors around, so no-one needs to suffer in silence. Why not take time to explore the possibilities, if this is your reality?

Happiness - A good woman

When we're not on the road giving presentations for Activate, we spend a lot of our waking hours researching women's issues by reading newspapers and magazines.

An article in Observer Woman (11/06/06), entitled 'What makes women happy', concludes with the following:

'So what does a happy woman look like? She's probably in a romantic, generous relationship; is surrounded by family she is fond of, or by friends; works part-time or for herself and has plenty of autonomy and control over her time; is involved in the community; has activities or projects outside herself which are consuming and which provide her with a sense of flow; is physically active and has a more or less spiritual sense of something valuable beyond herself.

Contrary to everything we're told by the self-help books, the key to happiness is not to examine your innermost self, to study your soul and think of yourself as a project to be worked on and enhanced. We are most likely to be fulfilled and so happy, by getting involved in something bigger than ourselves – a campaign, a love affair, family, a garden, writing, art. Happiness, it seems, is losing yourself in something or someone else.'

An interesting observation, we thought. Many of us have role models, heroes or someone we look up to and think 'I wish I could be like her.' Maybe we even think if we had all their qualities, our lives would be easier or better.

Our personal heroine is a nameless woman who's mentioned in the middle of the Bible. *The Message* version of the Bible describes her like this:

Proverbs 31

A good woman is hard to find and worth more than diamonds.

Her husband trusts her without reserve and never has reason to regret it.

Never spiteful, she treats him generously all her life long. She shops around for the best yarns and cottons and enjoys knitting and sewing.

She's like a trading ship that sails to faraway places and brings back exotic surprises.

She's up before dawn, preparing breakfast for her family and organizing her day.

She looks over a field and buys it, then, with money she's put aside, plants a garden.

First thing in the morning, she dresses for work, rolls up her sleeves, eager to get started.

She senses the worth of her work and is in no hurry to call it quits for the day.

She's skilled in the crafts of home and hearth, diligent in homemaking.

She's quick to assist anyone in need, reaches out to help the poor.

She doesn't worry about her family when it snows; their winter clothes are all mended and ready to wear.

She makes her own clothing and dresses in colourful linens and silks.

Her husband is greatly respected when he deliberates with the city fathers.

She designs gowns and sells them, brings the sweaters she knits to the dress shops.

Her clothes are well made and elegant and she always faces tomorrow with a smile.

When she speaks she has something worthwhile to say and she always says it kindly.

She keeps an eye on everyone in her household and keeps them all busy and productive.

Her children respect and bless her; her husband joins in with words of praise:

"Many women have done wonderful things, but you have outclassed them all!"

We'd love to think we could emulate her lifestyle consistently. We reckon that she manages to balance all of the eight areas covered in this book really well.

Our favourite phrase in the passage is, 'She's like a trading ship, sailing to faraway places bringing back exotic surprises.' We think there is such a sense of adventure, excitement and a little bit of mystery about this.

Q Did any of it resonate with you?

Q What was your favourite phrase? Write it here as a reminder.

Ten steps to happiness

Have you noticed how much discussion there is now about happiness?

One newspaper recently reported that eleven-year-olds in state schools are to be given lessons in happiness to help reduce stress and anti-social behaviour; there are TV programmes and countless articles in newspapers and magazines about the subject.

A recent social experiment was launched by Netmums (www.netmums.co.uk) to show that mothers could lead a fulfilling life if they followed ten simple principles for daily living.

1. COUNT YOUR BLESSINGS

2. HAVE A LAUGH EVERY DAY

3. DO A GOOD TURN

4. TREAT YOURSELF EVERY DAY

5. HALVE YOUR TV VIEWING

6. SAY HELLO TO A STRANGER

7. LOOK AFTER SOMETHING YOU'VE PLANTED

8. GET PHYSICAL

9. PHONE OR TALK TO A FRIEND

10. HAVE AN HOUR'S CONVERSATION WITH A GOOD FRIEND OR PARTNER.

'MAY YOU ALWAYS HAVE ENOUGH HAPPINESS TO KEEP YOU SWEET; ENOUGH TRIALS TO KEEP YOU STRONG; ENOUGH SUCCESS TO KEEP YOU EAGER; ENOUGH FAITH TO GIVE YOU COURAGE; AND ENOUGH DETERMINATION TO MAKE EACH DAY A GOOD DAY.'

Proverb

Why not try this yourself? For the next month, try and incorporate the following ten principles into your daily life and see what difference it makes to you.

With all this talk of happiness, there's a danger that we'll spend our lives thinking 'When I've done this, I'll be happy' or 'When that event is over, I'll be happy.' Maybe we believe that if the house was tidy, the underwear drawer was sorted, wardrobe colour co-ordinated, then we'd be happy. The reality is that none of these things is going to be the magic formula that will change our lives. However, we can take some steps towards improving our lifestyle and environment.

Wishful thinking

'The Three Wishes' project (www.3wishesforthefuture.com) was set up by Alex McKie and through it she invited people to make three wishes. She then travelled around the UK, and further afield, to find out what people were wishing for.

Her instructions were:

Wish for yourself
(even if you also wish well for others)

Follow your heart's desire
(your head may mislead you)

Be specific and definite
(then you're more likely to notice when your wishes have come true)

Q If you had three wishes what would they be?

_____

_____

_____

The act of just writing them down might be the first step to fulfilling something that's been on your mind for a long time.

Sometimes when we verbalise things, they take on a life of their own and have much more chance of taking place, than if we just keep thinking about them vaguely as something we'll do in the future. You could get together with a few friends over a few drinks and each share your three wishes and then begin to help each other to see how they might become a reality.

One Life Live

We only have one life to live so we need to live it to the full. If you're not happy with the way yours is going, it's great to get inspiration from others who have felt the same and made changes.

2006 saw the first attempt at an event to draw together in one place lots of people offering inspiration and solutions to boredom and inertia. Whether you dream of becoming your own boss or want to take a career break to travel or volunteer, if you long to relocate overseas or retrain for a new career, or if you simply feel in need of achieving a more fulfilling life – try a visit to this exhibition which now takes place annually in March. We've tried to encourage them to do a northern version but so far they are only concentrating on Olympia. It is well worth a visit: **www.onelifelive.co.uk**

Real life
- you are never too old to change!

Their fathers and mothers wound down gently into a quiet retirement, but today's over-fifties have no intention of following suit. They want to go on having it all, from travelling the world to preserving their looks, so says a new report from the think-tank Demos. Today people are determined not to be forced into retirement, consider old age begins after eighty rather than at 65 and have unconventional plans for their 'golden years'.

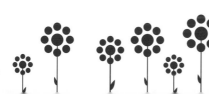

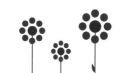

Life Begins at '??'

Put whatever number you choose in here – it's all relative!

We love this quote from Sheila Hancock and hope that when we reach our seventies, we'll be thinking in the same way.

'According to Psalm 90, my time is up. I've had my three score years and 10 plus a bonus of two. There is a get-out clause, though. I can make it to four score 'by reason of strength.' Which is why at 8am today I was lying backwards on a big blue ball levering two weights over my head. I loathe exercise. But it has to be done. I am waging war against gravity. The most natural thing at my age would be to yield to the pull, lie down and give up. So why don't I?

With the finishing post in sight, I have never been so desperate to relish every minute of life. In recent years, my husband and two dear friends, all younger than I, have had life wrested from them. In deference to them, I will value mine...

On my bedside table is a copy of The Power of Now. The past is over, the future limited, but right now I am here, lucky beyond measure and full of life. I used to be fearful. There was a lot to lose, I suppose. Now I have made friends with loss, I am less afraid...

Psalm 90 invites us to 'number our days that we may apply our hearts to wisdom.' OK I'll do a bit of that. But I prefer the Quaker advice to 'live adventurously'... My last lap is going to be hair-raisingly exciting!'

(Daily Telegraph August 13th 2005, p.2 Cover Story)

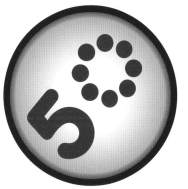

Sheila Hancock features on the cover of *Grumpy Old Women* the best-selling book by Judith Holder,[3] written as a follow-up to 'Grumpy Old Men' TV series. Mugs, T-shirts, the lot are now available as a generation of men and women relate to the honest humour of the 'Grumpies'.

Grumpy Old Women is written for women of a certain age, who not only have to multi-task and learn to cope with their changing bodies, but may have to cope with their own grumpy old men as well. The book covers the gamut of life's experiences and concludes with the following on the final page.

'Maybe some good old-fashioned religion would be helpful, some straightforward rules to live by instead of all this flailing about, trying to make some sense out of why we're here and what happens to us when we're gone... As I get older I get more and more receptive to religion. I like 'Thought for the Day' on the radio and I find myself enjoying stirring hymns – don't even turn them off any more. But being a Christian is so – well, unfashionable. You can be a Buddhist, feng shuist or whatever they call themselves, you can go around in orange robes and jangle cubes of crystal round your neck and people will give you some respect, but if you say you're a Christian you're written off as a nerd or an eccentric. But at the risk of sounding very old-fashioned indeed, I think if we all lived by Christian values, the world might be a considerably nicer place.'

We say Amen to that!

Talkback - Wants or needs?

Are you enjoying life? What drives you? How would you rate your current level of satisfaction and fulfilment?

These are important questions, according to Oliver James in his recent book, Affluenza:How to be successful and stay sane.[4] On a comprehensive study tour of seven countries, he encountered numerous examples, especially in the English-speaking nations, of people placing too high a value on money, possessions, appearances and fame. These were chased by full-on, frantic lifestyles.

American psychologist Erich Fromm has defined this as the Marketing Character (MC). Such people regard themselves as having fluctuating value, just like a product or a service, dependent on the approval rating and acceptance of those they need to impress.

Employers exacerbate this by using psychological tests to see if the attributes offered fit the company style. Even Personnel departments have changed to Human Resources – confirming that staff are another category of tools the firm owns to use for advancement.

Personal relationships are seriously affected once you go down this route. Friends or partners are weighed up for career purposes or to help confirm identity; looks, wealth or charisma count rather than intrinsic human value or plain old love.

The net result is the payment of a very high price. Seeking success before all else carries the risk of depression, anxiety, addictions and mental illness. When you only rate achievements and results, you cannot enjoy the processes and people along the way. Intimacy, love, belonging and security begin to fade – ironically the very areas we need in order to be successful and stay healthy.

Check your own rating by these few questions:

Q Do you choose something for what it looks like or because it is good value?

Q Do you always try to be in the right circles or relate equally with everyone?

Q Do you constantly seek more, better things, or are you content with what you have?

Q Does success feed your happiness or are you normally happy enough?

Q Do those who know you best think you are secure, loving and fulfilled?

Q What role model are you setting for children and others?

Q How would you describe the attributes needed to be successful?

HAZEL GAYDON

For Discussion

Q What constitutes success for which you strive in your own life?

Q Can we ever hope for change to our workaholic, materialistic society?

Q How many MC people do you recognise around you?

Q How can we be more authentic people at home and work and socially?

There could be lots of ways to finish this section on Personal Growth – but we like the words of the Mark D. Sanders and Tia Sillers song, 'I Hope You'll Dance'. Ronan Keating successfully recorded the lyrics in 2006 and it's always better to hear it sung than to read the words, so tap the song title into a search engine, like Google and sit back, enjoy the performance and plan how you'll choose to dance whenever there's a choice.

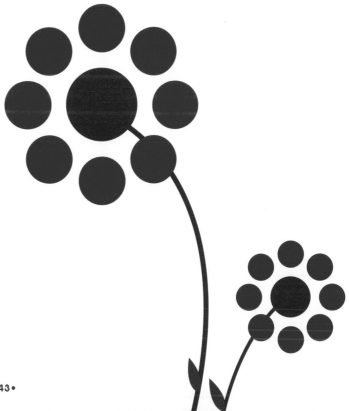

Life Laundry

Ruth is a self-confessed minimalist. If you sit around for too long in her house, you'll get dusted (just kidding – she's very hospitable really!) whereas you'd probably have to stand up at Jan's because the chairs are all full of books, newspapers and dogs.

Some of us, like Jan, can happily live in clutter and chaos, feeling that life's too short to spend too long on cleaning and tidying up. Others, like Ruth, can only function if they feel their home and workplace are organised and under control.

If clutter isn't a problem to you, then skip this section; it's not for you. The aim of this book isn't to make you feel you have to consider changes in areas where you're perfectly happy. However, if the mess around you is causing you stress, then it's time to make some changes.

When clutter seems to control you and take over your life, then it can be easier to block out the problem rather than deal with it. Maybe there just doesn't seem to be time to deal with the chaos.

For some, a structured plan to tackle the problem over a short period of time may work, whereas for others a few days and outside help may be needed to sort things out. The problem today is that we are bombarded with adverts, which tell us we're worth it, we deserve it and we just keep accumulating more and more.

If we look at the wider world, how many people cannot enjoy simple earthly pleasures like clean air, beautiful land or real freedom, because others relentlessly pursue more, bigger, better things? Enough is never enough.

Stuff does weigh us down. It can stop us making progress and reaching our goals and with it a far more serious type of clutter can begin to develop. It is the clutter we hold in our minds and thinking. We pick up messages all around us about the importance of things and absorb them without even noticing.

It starts when we are really young – we are almost trained in it. 'If you are a good girl when I'm shopping you can choose a toy.' Or, 'Be good for granny and mummy and daddy will bring back something nice for you.' Or even, 'What will you ask Father Christmas to bring you?'

So we begin to associate all aspects of life with what we will get from it. Then we mark achievements or certain ages with things: 'Now you are old enough to: have a TV in your room/buy make-up/have stuff'. Even the adverts tell us we get things 'because you're worth it'.

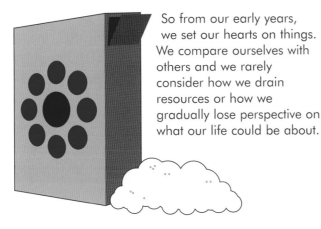

So from our early years, we set our hearts on things. We compare ourselves with others and we rarely consider how we drain resources or how we gradually lose perspective on what our life could be about.

Q Which of your possessions are most important to you?

Q If your house was on fire, which three things would you rescue?

So, let's quickly go around an imaginary house.

Lounge

What does it say about us? Books to look intellectual, videos we'll never watch, newspapers and magazines we'll never read? Do we need them all? Maybe our de-cluttering could take the form of buying *The Week* for a while and cancelling the papers, which can pressurise us into reading them. Ruth has started to throw all the newspapers into the recycling bag every evening, whether they've been read or not, so they don't build up.

Q What would an interior designer say about your lounge?

Q What would a woman from Darfur think?

Q How do you spend your time in this room?

Q Are others welcome?

Kitchen

Most of us have cupboards full of gadgets we'll never use, yet still get tempted to buy even more. But maybe the most important message for us in this room is the three R's: Reduce packaging, Reuse and Recycle.

Dining Room

Many homes don't have a separate dining room but wherever we eat, we feel that the new government initiative to get families to eat together is good. Is it realistic, though, to expect everyone to be in the same place at the same time, every evening? Perhaps your family meal could be eating breakfast together, maybe just once a week. If you live alone, you might decide to invite a friend or colleague to join you for a meal occasionally.

Q Think of one change you could make in this area and write it here.

Bathroom

Storing all those bits and pieces including magazines (if you're like us and use the bath to catch up on your reading) in baskets can transform a cluttered bathroom.

Q And when you look into the mirror in here, what do you see?

Q Are you happy with it?

Q Do you have a good self image?

Q If not, what steps could you take to improve it?

Maybe it's not looks, but health issues that worry you. Perhaps you're always asking 'What if?'. Are there changes you could make to work towards a healthier lifestyle?

Study

Few of us will have a study but most homes will have books and, often, too many to store easily. Some people buy too many shoes: we both buy too many books and Ruth realised a while ago, as she tried to get yet another boxful into the loft, that most of the books she had would never be read again.

She found it difficult at first, as she started to sort her books into a box for the charity shop. but soon got into the swing of it and hasn't missed those which have been passed on.

Bedroom

The popular wisdom is to sort out anything you haven't worn for twelve months and to give it to the charity shop and this is good advice. Could you have a sale or clothes swap with friends or with the other mums from school? Ask a friend in to help you clear out your wardrobes. This always makes it easier and more fun and then offer to do the same for her. Letting go of 'stuff' can feel good and you may find the extra space created makes your bedroom a space to relax and be calm.

Children's Room

Most parents agree that these rooms need a regular sort out, so plan to make the clear out a fun project, a game maybe with prizes. Buy cheap coloured boxes for different toys and encourage children to give away unwanted items to a good cause. A good principle is to give away a toy for every new one acquired.

Utility Room

Those of us who have a caring role or are responsible for the welfare of others can find this draining at times and it can prevent us from keeping on top of things. As women there can be a tendency for us to think we have to do everything, yet one third of us employ help of some sort in the home. Ruth has someone who does her ironing every week and will also child-mind and child-sit too. She wonders how she would manage without her. Others find that simply delegating tasks can take the pressure off.

Garden

Some people simply love tending a garden and feel that conquering the weeds and bringing order to a flower bed is great therapy. So why not try taming that wild patch at the bottom of the garden and plant some wild flower seeds? Most of us sit in the garden and this may represent the place to slow down, take stock and reflect on what life is all about. For some people, even if the home is uncluttered, their life feels out of control.

Q What are the three top priorities for your life right now?

Q Would the people close to you know that from the evidence of your life?

Q Is clutter in your thinking stopping you from building the life you were meant to enjoy? If so then what could you do about?

Q Are you paying enough attention to who you are inside? Or to why you are here?

Q Does your mind hold on to anxieties that haven't been addressed?

Q Or unhappiness from the past?

Q Or discomfort from a situation you are in at the moment?

Q Or guilt about yourself or others?

De-clutter your life

Q List ten things (non human) you wish you could remove from your life

Q How and where you will dispose of the goods or attitudes.

Q Put a timescale on eliminating three of them

'YOU CAN ONLY BECOME TRULY ACCOMPLISHED AT SOMETHING YOU LOVE. DON'T MAKE MONEY YOUR GOAL. INSTEAD, PURSUE THE THINGS YOU LOVE DOING, AND THEN DO THEM SO WELL THAT PEOPLE CAN'T TAKE THEIR EYES OFF YOU'

Maya Angelou

Environment

Green issues used to be seen as belonging to an alternative and even vaguely hippy lifestyle.

Now environmental awareness is a stark reality, with everyone being challenged to reduce, re-use and re-cycle.

We can all, as individuals, take it upon ourselves to reduce our own impact by thinking carefully about and trying to change the way we live – the way we travel, work, consume, enjoy our leisure, provide food, energy and shelter and dispose of our waste.

A very popular phrase for this is that we should leave a very light 'footprint' on the planet. Rowan Williams, the Archbishop of Canterbury, has taken a strong lead on this as he believes it to be a biblical stance:

'The Lord God placed the man in the Garden of Eden to tend and care for it.' Genesis 2:15

But caring for the planet is the responsibility of everyone who lives and breathes on it. A more environmentally responsible and sustainable lifestyle is not only less expensive in almost every way, but also more enjoyable. There are lots of easy-to-read books to help you out.

One of our personal favourites is *I count – Your Step-by-Step Guide to Climate Bliss* written by The Climate Movement.[5] This light-hearted pocket-sized book takes away any thoughts that we are helpless as individuals to make a change. You can read it in the bath: we did!

'ONE GENERATION PLANTS THE TREES; ANOTHER GETS THE SHADE'. **Chinese Proverb**

Lifestyle Choices

Power Supplies

Switch to 'Green Juice'. This means that whatever electricity you use is bought from renewable energy sources.

Harvesting Rainwater

Tubs for catching rainwater have been available for years and provide a ready supply of water for flower tubs, car-washing etc. Catching rainwater is not a new idea; our ancestors could have given us detailed instructions on how to do it.

Think about those people who have to walk miles simply to collect a bucket of water and then carry it back to their home. Why not distribute some leaflets in your area about WaterAid? WaterAid is an international charity dedicated to helping people escape the stranglehold of poverty and disease caused by living without safe water and sanitation. www.wateraid.org

Composting

Traditionally, gardeners have created their own compost using leaves, grass, shrub clippings and other useful materials found in the garden. Applying compost to soils provides an excellent conditioner and mulch, to fertilise and provide soil structure, retain moisture and can restrict weed growth. This is great news for gardeners.

In the UK around thirty million tones of domestic refuse is produced each year which contains an average of about 38 per cent organic content such as vegetable peelings, tea bags and food scraps. So don't dump it, recycle it. Bins are available at most DIY stores.

Allotments

If you are longing to grow your own food but you live in a flat or only have a small paved area outside your house, then you might have to settle for container gardening. Ask at the local garden centre about salad hanging-baskets.

Alternatively, you could offer to look after the garden of someone who can't manage to care for it – and share the produce. That way you'd be offering a lovely service and some much-needed company to a housebound person, getting some fresh air and exercise and eating the fruits of your labours.

You might even like to ask about the possibility of renting an allotment. Allotments are now a different world from the flat cap and whippet image that they have suffered from in the past. Renting one is not only an inexpensive way of getting your hands on valuable gardening space but also a great opportunity to meet fellow gardeners and a relaxing, sociable way to garden. It's a whole new world and, if they've got a bartering system in operation, you can trade excess produce with others.

Jan has four hens in her garden. Apart from being very cute and welcoming her visitors, they each lay one beautiful mahogany brown egg a day, which have lovely golden yolks. Visiting children love going to the nesting box and collecting them – especially if they are allowed to take them home.

Think about whether you can join the latest trend and keep a few garden hens or how about bee-keeping? Bees are crucial to maintaining the balance of the planet and honey is the most fabulous health and beauty product.

Organic food is great, but check how many miles its travelled to your plate!

Why not take a look at the River Cottage website for more clues about food choices. www.rivercottage.net

Recycling

When you finally do get around to deciding what things you can do without – why not recycle or Freecycle them? Freecycling websites are in operation around the world with the intention of matching up people to items. The only stipulation is that you must be willing to give your item away freely. To find out the Freecycling community in your area, log onto uk.freecycle.org

Home Planet

Radio 4 began the New Year in 2007 with the following Thought for the Day. We think it was a great start and that care of the planet should be on everyone's New Year resolution list,

'New Year is a time of beginnings, but if we don't heed the environmental warnings sounded on this programme, it could be another staging post towards the end.

In fact, if one were to write a Bible for the twenty-first century, it would start not like the old one with Genesis, the story of how God created the world, but with a kind of Genesis in reverse; how we dismantled it. And it might run like this:

In the end, human kind systematically demolished the home God had given them even though they had nowhere else to go. They plundered the earth and slaughtered their brothers and sisters of the animal kingdom. And this was the seventh day from the end.

They polluted the clear air with the fumes of their machines, poisoned the sea with their garbage and turned rivers into foaming torrents of chemical waste and began ever so slowly to choke themselves to death. And this was the sixth day from the end.

They stifled all truth that wasn't their truth and scoffed at the warnings of the prophets and were deaf to the ominous sounds of the earth in torment. Arrogance and self-righteousness drowned out wisdom and humility. And this was the fifth day from the end.

And they said the strong are entitled to most of what's going and the weak can have the rest. But the more they had to lose, the more they feared those who had nothing to lose, so they built ever bigger walls and larger armies to protect their self-interest. And this was the fourth day from the end.

They slept uneasily and awoke afraid and set to work to create the ultimate weapon. Then they said, 'Now we feel safe!' But their enemies didn't feel safe, so they too created an ultimate weapon and the whole world lived under the shadow of extinction and called it peace. And this was the third day from the end.

Then having proved by their cleverness that they could make anything, they said, now let us make God in our own image, let us gaze into a mirror and worship the one we see there. And this was the second day from the end.

And they were mesmerised by the gleaming products of their ingenuity and they cried 'Bigger! Faster! Stronger! Richer! Louder! More!' And they became frantic with a desire nothing could satisfy. And this was the day before the end.

Then there was chaos and uproar and when the din subsided, human life had vanished. And the ravished earth rested on the seventh day. Then God broke the silence. 'Back to the drawing board,' he said sadly.'

Rev Colin Morris[6]

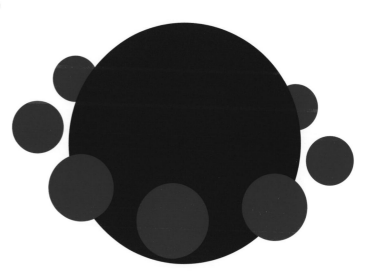

Talkback - How green are you?

Going green is no longer an option just for the ecologically aware minority. If our planet is to serve future generations well, we need to take measures now to preserve it.

Our use of energy is increasing along with our multiple appliances and acquisitions. The 'must-haves' of the twenty-first century, from the necessities to the novel, from business to pleasure, can result in bigger energy bills. More importantly, these symbols of western wealth can also speed up climate change.

Before we can lay the charge for this at the big corporations, or at the developers whose sustainable philosophy is growing at a slower rate than their profit margins, we need to start looking at our own lifestyle decisions.

If this is a matter of concern to you, as it must be for us all, use this quick check-list now to see how well you are doing to cut down carbon dioxide emissions at home.

Q Do I leave any electrical appliances on stand-by when not in use?

Q Do I have the heating on higher than I need?

Q Do I wear warm clothing rather than switch on a heat source?

Q Have I researched or installed any alternative energy methods?

Q Are draught-excluders fitted to all doors and windows?

Q Have I insulated lofts, roof spaces, water tank and pipes, floors, walls?

Q Could I reduce the water temperature to around 60 degrees?

Q Could I take a quick shower instead of running a full bath?

Q Do I know how to re-use washing water for the garden?

Q Am I re-cycling as much waste as I can?

Q Do I buy products which are eco-friendly?

Q Am I aware of the benefits of rainwater harvesting, geo-thermal heating or solar panels? Would they be an option for my home?

For every step we take in these seemingly small matters, the effect will be multiplied if we all do it – and our children's children may be able to continue to take pleasure in and on our wonderful planet Earth. Now there's a gift worth passing on!

For discussion

Q Are you worried about global warming?

Q Does your concern make you want to make changes like those listed already?

Q Would your home pass the energy performance test?

Q Could government give more incentives to save energy consumption?

Q Why should we care about the future of our planet?

HAZEL GAYDON

MY LIFE / WORK BLEND

The Mexican Fisherman

There are numerous versions of The Mexican Fisherman story on the internet, but whichever one you read, they all make the same point.

An investment banker was at the pier of a small coastal Mexican village when a small boat with just one fisherman docked. Inside the small boat were several large yellow fin tuna. The banker complimented the Mexican on the quality of his fish and asked how long it took to catch them.

The Mexican replied, 'Only a little while.'

The banker then asked why didn't he stay out longer and catch more fish.

The Mexican said he had enough to support his family's immediate needs.

The banker then asked, 'But what do you do with the rest of your time?'

The Mexican fisherman said, 'I sleep late, fish a little, play with my children, take a siesta with my wife, Maria, stroll into the village each evening where I sip wine and play guitar with my amigos, I have a full and busy life.'

The banker scoffed, 'I am a Harvard MBA and could help you. You should spend more time fishing and with the proceeds, buy a bigger boat. With the proceeds from the bigger boat, you could buy several boats. Eventually you would have a fleet of fishing boats. Instead of selling your catch to a middleman, you would sell directly to the processor, eventually opening your own cannery. You would control the product, processing and distribution. You would need to leave this small coastal fishing village and move to Mexico City, then LA, and eventually NYC where you will run your expanding enterprise.'

The Mexican fisherman asked, 'But, how long will this all take?'

To which the banker replied, 'Fifteen to twenty years.'

'But what then?'

The banker laughed and said 'That's the best part. When the time is right, you would sell your company stock to the public and become very rich. You would make millions.'

'Millions. Then what?'

The banker said, 'Then you would retire. Move to a small coastal fishing village where you would sleep late, fish a little, play with your kids, take a siesta with your wife, stroll to the village in the evenings where you could sip wine and play your guitar with your amigos...'

When you put it like that, wearing yourself out to make a fortune makes no sense at all. So why does anyone do it?

We need to take the hint and adjust our life/work balance in order to build in some play time. Sometimes it can be easier to go with the flow of the familiar stress that we've become used to, rather than take positive steps to change the way things are.

Q Envisage how you'd like your work/life blend to look in six months time and begin to plan for these changes now.

With some creative thinking and brainstorming with others, there's often a way around a seemingly insurmountable problem.

If you're looking for inspiration from others who have taken life changing decisions, then read Po Bronson's *What Should I Do With My Life?*.[7] When he was asked how he thought most people answered this question, he replied in an interview on his website,[8]

'Most attempt to answer it with one eye open, one eye closed. We let our fears govern our decisions; rather than challenging the validity of those fears:

we accept the boundaries set by those fears and end up confining our search to a narrow range of possibilities... we confine ourselves to a range that is acceptable to our parents or our spouse; we confine ourselves to places inhabited only by people 'like us,' meaning of our class and education level; we place too much emphasis on being respected by an imaginary audience...

I was inspired by people who had overcome these fears to look beyond the obvious choices. It wasn't easy for them, but in a way that hard journey made the result even sweeter. It wasn't just a matter of finding the right puzzle piece to match their skills; they had to grow as a person first.'

His website also has sample chapters of the book, interviews and other helpful information which would be of interest to anyone looking to make changes in their own life/work blend.

'IT IS BETTER TO WEAR OUT THAN TO RUST OUT.' Bishop Richard Cumberland

'THEY SAY **HARD WORK** NEVER HURT ANYBODY, BUT I FIGURE WHY TAKE THE CHANCE?' Ronald Reagan

BY THE SEVENTH DAY GOD HAD FINISHED THE WORK HE HAD BEEN DOING; SO ON THE SEVENTH DAY HE RESTED FROM ALL HIS WORK. AND GOD BLESSED THE SEVENTH DAY AND MADE IT HOLY, BECAUSE ON IT HE RESTED FROM ALL THE WORK OF CREATING THAT HE HAD DONE.

Genesis 2:2-3

Working to live or living to work?

What would be your ideal job? Probably one where you enjoy what you do, where you feel valued, where you use your talents, you work in a positive and supportive environment with people you like and where you are stretched – but not stressed.

Q Do you feel like that? If not, maybe it's time to make some changes.

Q What do you think your main skills are? (List everything: like being organized, relating to people, listening, cooking etc)

Q How could you translate them into your working day?

Q Would you like to do something completely different to earn your living?

Q Dream some dreams – write a list...

We found Po Bronson's book inspirational, as we read about more than fifty ordinary people who made their dreams a reality and there's plenty of practical advice within its pages.

Working from home

Drive down almost any motorway in the country and you'll spot signs in fields about the benefits of working from home. New technology such as the internet has enabled many people to work from home and some people see this as the ideal.

We both do this and while it has its advantages, there's always the temptation not to switch off at the end of the working day and allow work time to encroach on leisure time. It's a continual battle for us both and we frequently find ourselves working through more evenings than we should.

It can also be a lonely life without the stimulation of other colleagues to 'bat ideas about' with, so keep in touch with others as much as possible by phone or email and listen to the radio for news, handy tips and, above all, humour.

Working Parents

If you're needing a little help in juggling the demands of work and parenting, Parentalk, a charity which supports parents has developed 'Parentalk at Work', which focuses on supporting and equipping working parents. As well as the book[9] *How to Succeed as a Working Parent*, the charity offers events in the workplace and parent coaching, in conjunction with The Parentalk Coaching Academy, for individuals and small groups. It might be that something like this might be helpful if you feel as if you're juggling too many things. Contact **www.parentalk.co.uk** for details of all their resources.

Downshifting

Carl Honoré, author of *In Praise of Slow – How a Worldwide Movement is Challenging the Cult of Speed*[10], says this: *'These days more and more of us understand that living in fast-forward is not really living at all. When every moment is a race against the clock, when we forget how to slow down, there is a price to pay.*

Our diet, health and work, our relationships and communities, all suffer. But thankfully there is an alternative to living like a roadrunner. It's called downshifting.'[11]

With the overwhelming success of Hugh Fearnley-Whittingstalls River Cottage TV series (Channel 4 and Discovery Lifestyle) and his cookery books, it is obvious that people are attracted by the concept of a simpler lifestyle.[12]

If downshifting and living a life of simple self-sufficiency is out of the question (or doesn't appeal) then there are lots of ways you can simplify your life. Tracey Smith from Dorset set up National Downshifting Week in April 2006 and a website, giving some useful tips in making lifestyle changes slowly and deliberately. Apart from living a healthier and happier lifestyle herself, Tracey has won some awards.[13]

She is now working in partnership with others around the world, including Fiona Lippey from Australia, who set up www.simplesavings.org.uk along with her husband because they wanted to encourage people to simplify their lifestyle and cut their budget in order to work less hours and have more leisure time to spend with their families.

By logging onto their site, you can pick up free charts and budgeting tips that you can pass onto others. Why not collect some of the hints and information available and set up an advice service to help stressed-out people in your area who are working hard because of money problems?

Q What are the main changes you'd like to make to your own working pattern?

'IN JAPAN EMPLOYEES OCCASIONALLY WORK THEMSELVES TO DEATH. IT'S CALLED KAROSHI. I DON'T WANT THAT TO HAPPEN TO ANYBODY IN MY DEPARTMENT. THE TRICK IS TO TAKE A BREAK AS SOON AS YOU SEE A BRIGHT LIGHT AND HEAR DEAD RELATIVES BECKON'.

Scott Adams

WORK HARD AND CHEERFULLY AT WHATEVER YOU DO,

AS THOUGH YOU WERE WORKING FOR THE LORD.

Colossians 3:23

THEN JESUS SAID, 'COME TO ME ALL OF YOU WHO ARE WEARY AND CARRY HEAVY BURDENS AND I WILL GIVE YOU REST.'

Matthew 11:28

Talkback - Life/Work Balance

One of the first things strangers will ask us at a party is 'What do you do?' The answer we give can be very revealing and is often an indicator of the way we value and define ourselves. It's said that no-one can make us feel inferior unless we give them permission and this seems to be one area in which many of us are vulnerable. 'I'm just a housewife' is a give-away. Others do voluntary work and enjoy it, yet feel apologetic when describing it because it is unpaid work. Yet payback does not have to be financial – if finances are not a problem then the social aspect of a job or the feeling that you are helping others is the ultimate reward.

Doing nothing is a waste of time and a drain of our energy. Working is healthy and therapeutic and what we are designed to do. The Shakers motto is 'Hands to work, hearts to God' and we think that's a good work ethic. Yet even God had a day off – the Bible tells us that on the seventh day he rested and that's a good principle to work on. The importance is the balance. We spend so much of our time working. In the UK alone, six million people work over 48 hours a week and one million work over sixty hours a week. Then housework, shopping, etc, gets stuffed into weekends, so life becomes a treadmill – sometimes in order to fund a lifestyle we then have no time to enjoy. Yet if we find a job we love we might find that we can live on less, because we are not compensating for unhappiness through the week by buying lots of things we don't need.

Actors have learnt to distinguish between their work and the paid job they might take in order to pay the bills, when they are not employed in a film or a play. But whatever form it takes, most of us would agree that the ideal world is one in which we find work that we love doing that supports us financially. It helps if we discover what that is as early as possible.

Our education system is geared around us making life-choices before we have enough experience or knowledge of ourselves to make informed choices. Teenagers select the subjects they want to take forward for further study and at the tender age of sixteen are expected to plan career choices. These choices can be heavily influenced by teachers who want to boost their course numbers, or parents who are desperate for their offspring to follow in their footsteps. Sometimes finances can dictate the future because going to university is out of the question. Local colleges and universities will often welcome mature students onto courses because of the stability and life experience they bring. It's never too late to retrain and life-long learning can be a significant factor to enjoying health and happiness throughout the whole of life.

For discussion

Q How many hours of your life do you spend working – this includes housework?

Q What do you think the difference is between working to live and living to work?

Q When you were very young – what did you want to be when you grew up?

Q Did you do it? If not, why not? Did you feel that people put you off and inhibited you in any way?

Q If success was guaranteed and money was not part of the equation – what would you do?

Q Is there a way in which you might bring those desires to life in an unexpected way? Perhaps by retraining or offering to work in a voluntary capacity until you've gained experience?

If you're discussing this as a group why not decide to be accountable to each other about not working as many hours and possibly even looking for a job you'd prefer?

MY WELL-BEING

My Well-Being

Well-being is a word that can encompass our physical and spiritual health. In an age where around a fifth of the population struggle with stress and depression, most people link well-being to happiness.

Most people would like to be a little happier, but many of the things we spend our time pursuing: wealth, status, the perfect body and more time, don't guarantee extra happiness. So what does? Research consistently shows that friends, family, community and a sense of purpose, essentially our involvement with other people, are the important things. Focusing on what's positive instead of what's wrong makes people feel better about their lives. Experts say that it is possible and not that hard to increase your sense of well being and ways of doing this include:

- Committing yourself to making subtle changes in your daily life

- Not overloading your to-do list

- Being grateful for what you have

- Spending time with people you love

- Getting a good night's sleep

- Strengthening your sense of gratitude

- Spending less time pursuing a higher salary and more time improving your family life or taking up a hobby

- Spending time with your best friend (or even chatting on the phone)

- Playing with your kids

- Spending an hour alone with your partner

- Exercising regularly – you could go for short jogs with your spouse or a friend or get in training for a charity walk

- Planning get-togethers with the important people in your life, the way you arrange your meetings at work or doctor's appointments. Why not try making a commitment to maintain relationships with your friends and designate Friday evenings for your partner or for a girls' night out?

Q How many things in this list are a regular part of your life?

Q Which of them are most important to you?

Q What would you have to do to make more of them a reality?

Research shows that happy people tend to have strong social networks and spend a lot of time cultivating them. Social relationships do not guarantee great happiness, but it doesn't seem to occur without them.

Q Are you happy with your social networks?

Q What steps could you take to improve them?

Timebank

If you're keen to help others in your community, take a look at www.timebank.org.uk.

It's a great resource for women who want to do something practical and have skills to share and also gives value to those who feel they have nothing to offer.

Timebanking can include anything from collecting prescriptions from the chemist for the housebound, befriending phone calls, to giving advice on digital photography or plumbing – there's always something someone can do to help others and the possibilities are endless.

It's cool to be kind

An article in *You* magazine[14] entitled 'It's cool to be kind', suggested that the secret of career success and personal satisfaction isn't ambition, confidence and connections but the oft-forgotten quality of kindness and says the following six steps will help. We were struck by how similar this advice is to some of the things Jesus said.

- **Actions speak louder. It's not the thought that counts, it's the deed.**
- **Don't look for rewards. Do what you can and trust for the positive effects.**
- **Be generous with praise.**
- **Share the glory.**
- **Give others your full attention.**
- **Go one better – go the extra mile.**

Putting some of these principles into practice could make a different to our own feelings of well-being.

'LIVE WITH INTENTION. WALK ON THE EDGE. LISTEN HARD. PRACTICE WELLNESS. PLAY WITH ABANDON. LAUGH. CHOOSE WITH NO REGRET. CONTINUE TO LEARN. APPRECIATE YOUR FRIENDS. DO WHAT YOU LOVE. LIVE AS IF THIS IS ALL THERE IS.'

Mary Anne Radmacher

'WHEN ONE DOOR OF HAPPINESS CLOSES, ANOTHER OPENS;

BUT OFTEN WE LOOK SO LONG AT THE CLOSED DOOR THAT WE DO NOT SEE THE ONE WHICH HAS BEEN OPENED FOR US.'

Helen Keller

Laughter

> **'A CHEERFUL DISPOSITION IS GOOD FOR YOUR HEALTH; GLOOM AND DOOM LEAVE YOU BONE TIRED.'**
>
> **Proverbs 17: 22 (The Message)**

The Readers Digest calls it 'Laughter, the best Medicine' and they're right. Thousands of years ago, when the book of Proverbs was written, the same advice was given. According to a new study by cardiologists at the University of Maryland Medical Center in Baltimore, laughter, along with an active sense of humour, may help protect you against a heart attack.

In the study, researchers compared the humour responses of three hundred people. Half of the participants had either suffered a heart attack or had undergone heart surgery. The other 150 were healthy, age-matched participants who did not have heart disease.

The results confirmed that people with heart disease were 40 per cent less likely to recognise humour or use it to get out of uncomfortable situations. They generally laughed less, even in positive situations, and they displayed more anger and hostility.

Dr. Miller, Director of the Maryland Medical Centre says, 'The ability to laugh, either naturally or as learned behaviour may have important implications in societies such as the U.S. where heart disease remains the number one killer. We know that exercising, not smoking and eating foods low in saturated fat will reduce the risk of heart disease. Perhaps regular, hearty laughter should be added to the list. We could perhaps read something humorous

'IT'S AMAZING WHAT YOU CAN ACCOMPLISH IF YOU DO NOT CARE WHO GETS THE CREDIT.'

Harry S Truman

'VARIETY IS THE SOUL OF PLEASURE.'

Aphra Behn

or watch a funny video and try to find ways to take ourselves less seriously. The recommendation for a healthy heart may one day be – exercise, eat right and laugh a few times a day.'

We're fortunate to share a similar sense of humour and we send each other jokes at intervals during the day and are continually forwarding outrageous emails which drop into our inboxes. It relieves the monotony of working in splendid isolation.

So that's the humour sorted. As for exercise, we both like a stretch in the fresh air. Ruth walks, swims and cycles and Jan's feet rarely touch the ground on the way out for a walk, as she's being literally towed along by four dogs to the woods at the back of her house.

'Eating right' is more of a challenge as neither of us loves cooking. However, we both recognise the nutritional value of chocolate so we're unlikely to waste away as we write this book.

Before...

Fill this in before reading the book, using our example on P.12

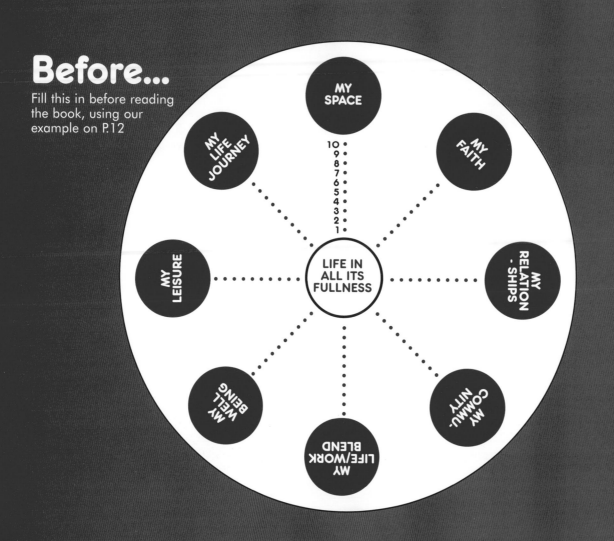

After...

Fill this in after you've read the book.

- MY SPACE
- MY FAITH
- MY LIFE JOURNEY
- MY RELATION-SHIPS
- MY LEISURE
- LIFE IN ALL ITS FULLNESS
- MY WELL BEING
- MY COMMU-NITY
- MY LIFE/WORK BLEND

10
9
8
7
6
5
4
3
2
1

Chocolate

One of our favourite 'feel good' products is chocolate and we both have lots of fridge magnets with comments like 'save the world – it's the only planet with chocolate.'

Smiling releases endorphins into the blood and so, apparently, does eating chocolate. So, provided you don't eat too much and make yourself feel sick, eating chocolate produces a sense of contentment and well-being.

Chocolate also has a dubious reputation as a sex substitute. We'll leave you to decide if that is true or not but here's a very sensual poem by Phil Isherwood who uses poetry and writing in therapy groups, which he calls 'writing for survival'...

Chocolate

No other substance
Has such an intimate relationship
With my taste buds.
The anticipation alone
Evokes the sweet passion of
Knowledge. I enjoy waiting, waiting,
For that deep dark taste.
I can promise myself, later,
When I've finished this,
When I've decided.
It's like unwrapping a moment
Untouched by time.

Smooth, hard and not-quite cold
To my lips.
The surface surrenders first, then
The giving smoothness,
A sensual melting into
The corners of my mouth.
Slowly all shape disappears
The physical abandoned, leaving
Pure experience to invade,
It seems, every cell in my body.

It may have been some time ago
That my eyes closed.
But as the world recovers its
usual pose
Around me, I find I look on
the world
With a new-found benevolence.
Perhaps... if I were to consider
Afresh each person I meet,
As possibly the very one
Who invented Chocolate?[15]

Anyway – keep on bringing it on is what we say!

As chocoholics, we love this Roald Dahl quote

'NEVER MIND ABOUT 1066 WILLIAM THE CONQUEROR, 1087 WILLIAM THE SECOND. SUCH THINGS ARE NOT GOING TO AFFECT ONE'S LIFE... BUT 1932 THE MARS BAR AND 1936 MALTESERS AND 1937 THE KIT KAT - THESE DATES ARE MILESTONES IN HISTORY AND SHOULD BE SEARED INTO THE MEMORY OF EVERY CHILD IN THE COUNTRY.'

We think chocolate is one of God's best ideas but, like so many of the best things in life, it's open to abuse. In certain parts of the world the workforce are treated like slaves and forced to work long hours for a pittance harvesting the chocolate they've never even tasted, in order to meet a growing demand from the West.

There's a lot of helpful information about Fairtrade on the website www.fairtrade.org.uk as well as stories about how it helps real people. Ovidia is one of them.

'Ovidia and her husband, Ovispo sell all of their cocoa to their farmers' association, a member of the Conacado farmers' co-operative. Less than half reaches the Fairtrade market, because as yet there is insufficient consumer demand. For this part of their crop, the farmers receive a guaranteed minimum price. The remaining cocoa is sold to the conventional market where prices have been very low, below the cost of production, for over two years. They have been earning an average of about 2,500 pesos a month which just about covers their

costs and allows them living expenses. There is no money left over, but if there was, Ovidia would like to save it to make improvements to their home.

The Fairtrade price has sustained them during long periods of low market prices. Sales to the Fairtrade market have enabled Conacado to set up a nursery, which supplies low-cost plants to the farmers, so they can grow most of their own food.'

So we would urge everyone to buy Fairtrade chocolate, which is now widely available. The Fairtrade website has an extensive list of UK suppliers of Fairtrade chocolate and where it can be bought.

'Chocolate doesn't make the world go round... but it certainly makes the ride worthwhile.'

'FUN IS FUN BUT NO GIRL WANTS TO LAUGH ALL OF THE TIME.'

Anita Loos

'HAPPINESS IS GOOD HEALTH

Ingrid Bergman

– AND A BAD MEMORY.'

'THE SUPREME HAPPINESS IN LIFE IS THE CONVICTION THAT WE ARE LOVED.'

Victor Hugo

Pampering

Beauty editors Sarah Stacey and Jo Fairley liken a woman to a garden, which needs tending to look its best. So they suggest having regular spa experiences and allowing yourself time to unwind in order to appreciate and enjoy them more – perhaps even booking appointments around key diary dates like birthdays to alleviate guilt.

Their bestselling book[16], *The 21st Century Beauty Bible*, contains lots of common sense about such things as avoiding absorbing harmful chemicals and they have used panels of women to test hundreds of products . They give recipes for home-made products and Jo has also written *The Ultimate Natural Beauty Book*.[17]

Janey Lee Grace's book *Imperfectly Natural Woman*[18] gives excellent advice on natural beauty products and ways to unwind.

Maybe you'd like an hour having the opportunity to give yourself a facial and try out a host of moisturisers, face packs and cleansers, all derived from natural Mediterranean products. You'll feel the difference immediately as these treaments leave your skin feeling refreshed and toned.

Temple Spa is a new range of products which is hitting spas and leading stores as well as 'spa at home' parties. We've both had Gill, the lovely Temple Spa organiser, come and hold parties in our homes and can vouch for the quality of their gorgeous products which can be found on their website, www.templespa.com

'THE IDEA OF ALWAYS BEING AT PEACE, ALWAYS BEING BLISSFULLY HAPPY IS SCARY. ANYONE IN A PLACID STATE IS JUST GOING TO VEGETATE.'

Joseph Heller

'THE HAPPIEST WOMEN, LIKE THE HAPPIEST NATIONS, HAVE NO HISTORY.'

George Eliot

'TO FILL THE HOUR – THAT IS HAPPINESS.'

Ralph Waldo Emerson

'I LIKE LONG WALKS.

ESPECIALLY WHEN THEY ARE TAKEN BY PEOPLE WHO ANNOY ME.'

Fred Allen

Talkback: The Good Body

In her play *The Good Body*, Eve Ensler tackles the theme of our current obsession to achieve the perfect shape. She is highlighting a search common to many these days, permeating all sections of society.

Along with being happy in relationships, successful in their careers and stylish in their homes, 21st century people aspire to be beautiful. Magazines, catwalks and celebrities parade the images which fuel the desire and push the standards ever higher.

A quick survey amongst your closest circle is bound to reveal a level of dissatisfaction with some aspect of each one's body. If the nose, chin, stomach, hips, legs, arms, breasts, feet could be smaller, larger, flatter, firmer, longer, shorter or smoother – we would all be gorgeous.

Many would admit to storing a wardrobe item simply waiting for the time our shape becomes what we long for it to be; others have creams or lotions designed to disguise the bad points; a few worry enough to undergo surgery to have body parts fixed or changed for good.

Modern women no longer face the strictures of corsets and liberty bodices – their problem is the vast choice of undergarments to enhance, not hide, their form. Beauty products, gym sessions, diet systems and image publications are a must in the monthly budget for many women, if they are to keep up appearances.

Fast-food feasts or five lots of fresh fruit? A winter walk or a warming fireside wilt? It is a daily battle of hard work, dedication and sacrifice if we want the perfect body. Will this national neurosis ever die down? Whole industries thrive on our anxiety to look right.

Yet denial of any interest in our image could indicate another type of imbalance. We can rightly enjoy making the best we can of the body we have.

It can be a lot of fun to pursue the odd pampering purpose with a friend and can help to alleviate the stresses of our fast paced lives.

Perhaps the answer lies within each of us, as we grow to appreciate one of life's secrets which is more than skin-deep.

It is 'inner beauty' that really gets us noticed. The Bible talks about inner beauty being more important than how we look on the outside and lists some fabulous qualities – **love, joy, peace, patience, kindness, generosity, faithfulness, gentleness** and **self control**, which, if we exhibit them, will ensure our inner beauty shines through.

Looking at this list

Q Which characteristics are evident in your life?

Q Which ones need to be developed?

For discussion

Q Is a good outward appearance important?

Q What is a balanced approach to personal beauty?

Q What is 'inner beauty'?

Q How is inner beauty best developed?

HAZEL GAYDON

MY LEISURE

Thirsty Thursday

'We must get together...'.How often have you said those words – and meant them – but somehow the meeting up never happens?

A small group of friends from Manchester found a way to solve this dilemma. They were busy businesswomen and friendships were getting neglected, so they made a point of putting a regular meeting in their diaries. From now on they would meet up for drinks and a chat after work on the last Thursday of every month.

Now Thirsty Thursday has a network of over five hundred women and their meetings range from a champagne afternoon tea at the five star Lowry Hotel to an after-hours fashion session at Harvey Nicks, with canapés in the restaurant and special privileges for those who stay to eat dinner. This expansion shows that meetings like this are of interest to busy women.

If life has become so busy that you are in danger of losing touch with some of your friends, then why not plan some creative space to get together?

Q Who would you invite?

Q When could you meet?

Q What creative things could you organise?

The words on the street

Poetry is losing its elitist image, with public jams and slams and websites.

As the demand for public literature events of all kinds have increased, so have the performing skills of most poets, and the performance scene is growing.

Pubs, arts centres, clubs, theatres and even art galleries now regularly host 'open mic' events, poetry slams in which the audience choose the winner.

Scottish groups have long enjoyed Burns night sessions but there may well be interest in your corner of the world for some culture. Make it fun, choose a comfortable venue, dress up – use good lighting and invite inspiring performers. This might well be an unexpected way of drawing people from across the generations together.

Of course, poetry can also be a glorious, peaceful, individual pastime. Lots of life coaches suggest reading something inspirational every day and we agree wholeheartedly. It may even make you look at the world differently.

Psalm 23:2&3

HE LETS ME REST IN GREEN MEADOWS;

HE LEADS ME BESIDE PEACEFUL STREAMS.

HE RENEWS MY STRENGTH.

Creativity/Hobbies

There is something about creativity that is good for the soul.

Watch a child finish their first picture or bake a batch of mis-shaped buns and cast your mind back to your own early achievements. A little bit of pride can build self-esteem and confidence.

We just love this stuff. Ruth does scrapbooking and Jan makes soap and cards and they are all great ways to unwind and gather the girls together. Jan was given a day course on soap making as a birthday present and that's how her interest started. Now she's got her own small business, 'As in Eden.' Take a look at www.asineden.co.uk to see how this simple gift has developed.

Time to kick the leaves isn't an easy option for many of us, yet there's something very satisfying about tapping into the creativity we all have and taking time to develop this.

Q Is there something you've always promised yourself you'd get around to doing? What is it?

Q What would you need to do in order to begin?

Scrapbooking

One of the most satisfying forms of creativity is to bring order out of chaos and make something of lasting beauty or value that others can enjoy.

One such activity that requires only basic skills and can be attempted by people of all ages is scrapbooking. Ruth does not consider herself to be naturally creative, but she has found that scrapbooking has given a real outlet for a latent creativity that must be lurking somewhere deep inside.

Scrapbooking is based on the idea that we've all got photos in carrier bags and boxes which we plan to put into albums one day. This hobby shows us how to display photos in amazingly different and creative ways. Classes are held around the country and as well as craft shops, stores like Lakeland now stock scrapbooking items. Children love it; new mums proudly begin their first child's album within days of the birth. Octogenarians derive huge pleasure from building up a 'memory' book to leave to their grandchildren and fostered and adopted children can find that 'life story' work becomes a pleasure, rather than a chore. Women who meet in a variety of situations continue to meet and scrap 'n natter, learning new techniques together.

One of the magazines devoted to scrapbooking recently carried the following on its letters page:

'Last Friday I went to buy a magazine to read on the train on the way home and picked up the first edition of your magazine.

I was so inspired that on Saturday I went to the local art & craft shop, stocked up on a few items and let my imagination run riot. By Sunday my first ever attempt was finished. I suffer from severe depression, but I got so engrossed in what I was doing that the time flew by and I ended up feeling relaxed and as though I had achieved something. Needless to say, I can't wait to get started on my next page – and I just wanted to say thank you, as this has done more for me in three days than 23 years of medication and counselling has.'

We wondered if scrapbooking is something that should be offered on the NHS. Once you've got the knack of scrapbooking, you'll never be stuck for ideas for an original gift for a special birthday or anniversary. A small album of personal photos all displayed in an original way is acceptable to everyone.

Film clubs

Film clubs are a great way to meet for a social event. They get the old brain cells going and hearing other people's points of view helps you to get more out of the experience.

Why not get a group together and do a block booking at the cinema, followed by a posh coffee or tapas? Or it could be a good night in with a DVD and supper. If everyone gets to choose a film, it also encourages you to watch a different genre of film than you might naturally choose. It'll widen your horizons. The website www.damaris.org lists suitable questions for discussion under its Culture Watch section for films and books.

For films to watch and discuss with younger members, containing no gratuitous violence and promoting positive values – contact Feature Films for Families 0845 6441630 www.familymovies.co.uk

Reading groups

Almost every magazine and newspaper features a Book of the Month and reading groups are said to be the fastest growing leisure activity in the country.

We were intrigued to read this comment in *The Times* by the author Jeanette Winterson about the power of a book;

'Good books are detonating devices, able to trigger something in the mind of the reader – a memory perhaps or a revelation, or an understanding not possible by other means. Not for nothing was Madame Bovary kept away from trapped French housewives.

The introverted nature of reading is part of its power. No-one knows what you are thinking as you read. No-one can see what changes might be taking place under the surface of your silent repose. It is this unaccountability to external authority that makes reading both defiant and an act of free will. The CCTV and the bugged phone can do nothing about the private dialogue between reader and writer.'[19]

A variety of different groups are emerging. Some are made up of mums and daughters who meet together for some serious bonding time as they discuss a favourite novel, whilst others are set up for all the members of the family to join together. One national newspaper has set up a family reading group and followed its progress over a period of time and found it to be hugely successful.

Some groups are a good excuse to get together and chat, while others have a particular focus and concentrate, for example, on cookery books or crime novels. If you're interested in joining a reading group ask at your local library, a bookshop, look in your local paper or consider starting your own. The internet has plenty of advice on how to begin.

Q What is your all-time favourite book?

Q Would it make a good discussion topic?

Q They say there is a novel in all of us
– What title would you give yours?

Talkback - Third Space

How might you connect a cycle ride, learning a language, visiting gardens, having a massage and taking a cookery course? A description of your weekend? These are just a few out of hundreds of possible leisure activities.

I wonder what you choose to do in what used to be called leisure time but sociologists have re-named 'Third Space'? For your choice about this indicates some interesting things about values and aspirations. Ask any slimming club member, jogger or short-break traveller and you will soon understand their priorities.

Some people now prize building memories over pursuing materialism. They don't want 'stuff' any more – they feel that their basic needs have been met and have lost interest in simply upgrading the car or the TV. Even trailing round shops to be tempted to buy no longer attracts them.

People increasingly want social experiences and this is borne out by the amount of money now spent in coffee shops, restaurants, sports clubs and theme parks; social places to meet others and opportunities not to be missed. So much so that we are now turning into an 'experience economy', forcing a change in marketing policies. You may have seen shopping malls now advertising themselves as a place for a day out: come to browse and dine and even catch a film – and of course shop if you feel like it. Bookshops are re-styled with comfy sofas and coffee bars and you are encouraged to stay around. There is a growing sense of hospitality, bringing an emotional connection with customers. The philosophy is to make ordinary products feel like an extraordinary experience.

Those who thought the key to happiness lay in the acquisition of the dream car or the healthy bank balance have realised that satisfaction does not come with those things – so now we search elsewhere for fulfilment. The Future Foundation tells us that personal fulfilment is now the top priority for 50 per cent of Brits. We see our lives as a project in progress; so we do new things, pick up new skills, grow vegetables, learn a language or do worthy deeds as we try to work out who we really want to be.

**The possibilities are endless.
One life-time hardly seems long enough.
Make the most of it while you can.**

For discussion

Q What fills your Third Space?

Q Do you prize experience over possessions?

Q Where are you looking for fulfilment at the moment?

Q If life is a project, what marks would you get so far?

Q How can we know the true value or success of our life?

HAZEL GAYDON

MY COMMUNITY

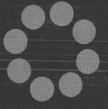

Community

A group of people living in one locality or having cultural religious, ethnic or other characteristics in common.

You have heard that the Law of Moses says, 'Love your neighbour and hate your enemy.' But I say, love your enemies! If you are kind only to your friends, how are you different from anyone else? Matthew 5:43-47

Community means many things. Mostly it refers to a geographical area or group who live around you. It can also refer to a group with whom you have a shared interest that might travel in from many directions, or colleagues at work who might be the people with whom you spend most of your waking hours.

It might describe the people around you at the gym or other place of leisure, at toddler group or the school gate or people you've begun to get to know a little and might be able to chat with. Ruth meets up with neighbours to go for a run, Jan is part of a craft group and we're both in reading clubs.

Q How would you define community?

Q What does it mean to you?

Q List the people that you consider to be part of your community.

Sometimes difficult circumstances might project you into a new community. Jan's uncle had a heart by-pass and he met up with others for walks to get the mandatory exercise. The men became close friends as a result of shared experiences and a mutual desire to get well and encourage each other.

A friend of Ruth's realised that her community was made up of the women she was having chemotherapy with, after surgery for breast cancer. Once their treatment was over, the women met up regularly for support and began to develop new hobbies together.

You might even belong to an online community and take part in online debates, an activity which is rapidly gaining in popularity. Read some of Jan's blog contributions on www.NewlyWeds-uk.com

Ruth is a co-ordinator for AdoptionUK and their online community provides a valuable support network for parents who often live hundreds of miles apart but who rely on the understanding and advice of others who may be facing similar challenges.

Belonging is important from a very early age, when most of us just want the freedom to do what others are allowed to do. That's why the teenage books with titles like Yvonne Coppard's, *Everybody else does! Why can't I?* (Puffin, 1994) strike a chord with us. We've all got embarrassing photographs of that unfortunate outfit that everybody was wearing that season (haven't we?) It's funny to see those fashions appearing again. As we said, life goes round in circles.

Q Do you tend to take it personally when people move out of your life for one reason or another?

Q Think of a time when this might have been a positive experience.

Often people get together because of a shared interest, but sometimes when that particular activity comes to a natural end, they find that they have little else in common and the group disperses.
So community tends to be informal and fluid and people drift in, stay for a while and then often move on and the phrase 'holding people on an open hand' is a good description. Sometimes moving to a new area means that we have to let go of some old relationships in order to make room for new ones.

When Ruth and her family moved to Sheffield six years ago, they didn't know anyone in the area. They bought their home on a new housing development and before long they were part of a new community. There were barbecues being planned, nights out at the local pub, girly trips to a spa and even a weekend away in London. A very natural community sprang up, just because everyone had moved into the cul-de-sac at the same time.

Jan lives in Leigh, a small town in the North West that once had a thriving cotton industry and several working coalmines. It's the sort of place where people live in the same house for sixty years and everyone knew your granddad. The local police inspector says it's one of the safest places to live in the north of England, but then again he might just be biased.

Whichever way you approach it, community is about belonging. It can establish our roots and sense of identity. As part of a community, we can experience rejection, loneliness and a feeling of 'other-ness' or we can feel accepted and valued. The latter experience can be crucial to our self-esteem and well-being.

Sometimes we can enhance the feeling of close community around ourselves with very little effort. Try finding out who delivers your post and your milk and greet them by name. Surprisingly, it makes you feel good too. Jan's postman, Jimmy, tries out all her new recipe soaps and home-made toiletries, which have had an amazing effect on his skin. He tells her that he now looks forty, which is a pity as he's only 27.

Seriously, when her elderly St Bernard dog wandered off, it was Jimmy who spotted him and brought him home.

I EXPECT TO PASS THROUGH THIS WORLD BUT ONCE; ANY GOOD THING THEREFORE THAT I CAN DO, OR ANY KINDNESS THAT I CAN SHOW TO ANY FELLOW CREATURE, LET ME DO IT NOW; LET ME NOT DEFER OR NEGLECT IT, FOR I SHALL NOT PASS THIS WAY AGAIN.

Stephen Grellet, Quaker Missionary

Neighbourliness

Hopefully you live in a friendly area too.

According to a Government general household survey, things are fairly friendly down your street. Around three-quarters of people believed that neighbours in their area looked out for each other and similar proportions had done a favour for a neighbour or had received a favour from a neighbour during the last six months. Just over half answered yes to all three of these questions.

In our last book *Unlocking the Door*[20] we tell the story of how a neighbourhood was changed simply because one couple had a MacMillan Coffee Morning. The neighbours enjoyed getting together and willingly joined in the Shoebox project with Operation Christmas Child. Each household made up a shoebox of gifts for a child and they were all sent to war-torn countries.

Since then there have been dinner parties, pamper sessions and barbecues and the neighbours have all started greeting each other by name and exchanging Christmas cards. It feels a much friendlier place to live now. The neighbours were already nice people; they just needed someone to get them all together.

Q What do you contribute to your local community?

Q Could you be the one to start something new in your area?

Q Do you know those who live round you well enough to know what would work?

Sadly, some people are still lonely and it's good to seek them out, especially at vulnerable times like Christmas, when it can seem as if everyone else is playing happy families.

Jan's family are used to having an assortment of people around the table on Christmas Eve. They consider it's what makes Christmas special and her kids now invite people themselves to join the party. Everyone brings some food and a wrapped gift to put in a sack for a Present Swap. But they also bring something special to the dynamics and friendships are made around the table. Sometimes the friendships develop and this year one couple got married.

Ruth and her neighbours are good at looking after each other's children, which is really helpful in a crisis, and often people will pop in just for a chat because they know they are guaranteed tea and sympathy. Sometimes being listened to is enough and then people can often see a way around their situation which seems much lighter for having been shared.

Through her involvement with adoptive families, Ruth is part of another community. Often the challenges faced by these parents are different from those of their friends and the support they find by spending time with others experiencing similar situations is really important. So she can regularly be found serving copious amounts of coffee and cake to other parents while the children enjoy playing with others of their own age who live in 'forever' families.

'I AM OF THE OPINION THAT MY LIFE BELONGS TO THE COMMUNITY, AND AS LONG AS I LIVE IT IS MY PRIVILEGE TO DO FOR IT WHATEVER I CAN'.

George Bernard Shaw

We'd like to ask you a few questions about the people who you value and remember. Can you name:

- The five wealthiest people in the world?

- Britain's first astronaut?

- Five winners of Miss World?

- Ten Nobel prize winners?

- Six BAFTA winners?

How did you do?

Try this instead. Can you list people who have inspired you in your life? Perhaps

Q Two good teachers from your school days

Q Three good friends

Q A mentor

Q People who made you feel appreciated and special

Q Five people you enjoy being with

Why not write to someone who has inspired you, to say thank you. A simple note saying 'I've never mentioned this, but ...' could be a real encouragement.

Q Who could you write to?

We can both think of women who were there for us throughout our lives, with advice, inspiration and encouragement. They weren't particularly wealthy but they were incredibly generous of spirit. Hopefully similar people will come into your mind as you read this. The next generation needs such women; could you be one of them?

Q What would you most like to be remembered for in your community?

Further reading

If you want some useful tips of how you can be a better neighbour, treat yourself to the book – *Change the World for a Fiver: we are what we do.*[21]

This book has been around for a while but it is a timeless reminder that 'we are what we do.' The book was printed to launch the community website www.wearewhatwedo.org and is filled with great suggestions and arty illustrations. One of the suggestions is to send a postcard (actually provided in the book) to thank someone for their impact on your life. Another idea is to rip out some strips from the book to put through doors introducing yourself to your neighbours.

Simply knowing the names of other people causes them to exchange things like Christmas cards and boosts community spirit.

Since the website was launched, the community team has worked with schools and businesses, made films, given lectures and translated their suggestions into three languages – proving that community spirit crosses all boundaries. People contact the

organisation to register a good deed and, at the time of writing, the counter was at 621463. That's a lot of lives made happier!

The same publishing company have now published another book titled *Change the World 9-5 : 50 ways to change the world at work.*[22] Why not put some of their suggestions into action to make a better world? At just £5 you could buy one for your friends for Christmas or birthday presents. Both books are available at various locations, including Oxfam shops.

'NEVER DOUBT THAT A SMALL GROUP OF THOUGHTFUL COMMITTED CITIZENS CAN CHANGE THE WORLD. INDEED IT IS THE ONLY THING THAT EVER HAS'.

Margaret Mead

Global Community

There are so many possible ways to help improve the lives of people in other countries, either by donating money to provide clean drinking water or by sponsoring a child to ensure that they have access to a regular hot meal and a good education.

Activate 'adopted' a charity called Achkiy a few years ago and we've been privileged to have made significant improvements to the lives of many families in the shanty towns of Lima in Peru.

Achkiy was set up by Julia Castle (daughter of Fiona and the late Roy Castle) as a response to the growing unemployment and poverty that occurred as many people moved from the rural areas into Lima searching for work. Unable to find jobs and with housing too expensive to afford, people set up homes on the hills surrounding Lima, without water or sanitation.

Initially teaching the women to make beautiful silver jewellery, Julia founded Achkiy to provide training, work and dignity for women in Peru. Over the past twelve years, Achkiy has grown and now makes recycled sugarcane husk paper notebooks and aluminium Christmas decorations, as well as cards and jewellery.

Funds are raised for Achkiy in a variety of ways. Some people simply invite a small group of friends in to watch a short DVD about the project and browse through a selection of hand made goods while others organise a stall at a local summer or Christmas fair. You can hold an Achkiy event yourself by contacting Julia at info@achkiy.com

'IN EVERY COMMUNITY THERE IS WORK TO BE DONE. IN EVERY NATION THERE ARE WOUNDS TO HEAL. IN EVERY HEART THERE IS THE POWER TO DO IT'.
Marianne Williamson

Fashion conscience

If you're like us, love clothes and enjoy bargain hunting, you might want to ask a few questions about just how your outfit could be produced at such a low price. Throwaway fashion is OK but what about the community of workers who spend hours stitching for a pittance?

Q How important do you think it is to consider the source of our purchases?

The Rough Guide to Ethical Shopping[23] is an excellent source of practical information if you want to think more about this whole issue. Their blurb states;

Shopping can sometimes seem like a moral minefield - which companies and products should we support or avoid? And which ethical claims can we trust? The Rough Guide to Ethical Shopping answers these and many other questions -

The Issues: Do boycotts work? Is buying local better? How fair is Fairtrade? What about third-world labour and oppressive regimes?

The Products: From tea to trainers, fish to furniture, pensions to plane tickets – the problems and the ethical options.

The Companies: Where to shop ethically: clothes and food stores, banks, travel agents and much more.

With recommended websites, books and magazines plus tips on how to do your own research, *The Rough Guide to Ethical Shopping* is the essential handbook for responsible consumers.

Swapping's the new Shopping

If you want to update your wardrobe but are concerned about buying yet more stuff, then why not join the increasingly popular trend for bartering not buying?

Forget the endless High Street queues for the newest range of clothes or rummaging in vintage or secondhand shops for an overpriced relic – the latest trend is swapping. From groups of friends hosting informal evenings in their homes offloading their cast-offs, to large, city-wide events and international internet based swaps – it's all the rage.

Lots of people find ebay is too much of a hassle when they want to downsize their wardrobe. Aware that perhaps their cast-offs are just too good for the charity shop and increasingly conscious of the ethical message to recycle, an alternative had to be found.

Frank Furedi, a professor of sociology at the University of Kent, said recently in one of the national newspapers that our wish to show that we care about the environment is certainly a factor in the popularity of swapping, but he believes that it's a very complex phenomenon that has more deep-rooted explanations. He said,

'Swapping is a far more interactive experience than shopping. It's about making contact with people, forging social relationships, making friends. Shopping is, on the whole, a transaction – something that demands very little interaction. But there's increasing evidence that people want shopping to be more of an experience; something that has meaning.'

To see how the professionals are doing it and pick up some great tips on hosting your own clothes swapping event, log on to www.y-shop.co.uk

Asylum Seekers

There is a way to help people who have actually had to flee from difficult situations overseas and have landed on these (often inhospitable) shores in order to preserve their lives from persecution, if not necessarily from hunger. If we are willing to listen, their stories will touch our hearts and many people have been spurred into action through the plight of asylum seekers in our neighbourhoods.

Is there a disadvantaged group in your community that you might have the time and skills to help? Something as simple as help with filling in forms can lift a burden from someone who is confused and stressed by their situation.

The Association of Visitors to Immigration Detainees (AVID) has an excellent website full of useful advice for anyone wanting further information – www.aviddetention.org.uk

We can all moan that the area where we live is not particularly friendly and there isn't a great sense of community. Change can happen when one person makes a simple suggestion that draws people together and promotes goodwill. Why not try it today? We can guarantee that your personal score in the Community section of the Life Circle will be boosted and the Relationships section might be hugely improved as well.

NO ACT OF KINDNESS,

HOWEVER SMALL,

IS EVER WASTED.

Aesop

WHEREVER THERE IS A HUMAN BEING,

THERE IS AN OPPORTUNITY FOR KINDNESS.

Seneca (Roman Philosopher)

Talkback - Fairtrade

International trade practices have meant economically strong nations and powerful companies have flourished at the expense of poorer, smaller producers. Fairtrade demonstrates how trade can be more favourable to poor people and the environment too. It guarantees farmers in developing countries a fair price, so they can cover costs and plan for the future. At present, more than five million people in 49 countries are able to benefit; and the range of available products is growing all the time. If you'd like more information about Fair trade, take a look at www.fairtrade.org

A coffee farmer in Tanzania says: 'Without our co-operative and selling to the Fairtrade market, our life would have been terrible. Fairtrade gives us hope and courage, we are able to earn enough to provide for our families.'

The constant price war has caused coffee shelf prices to go below the cost of production; so farmers are losing out, receiving a pittance for their valuable crop. When a fair price is paid, these producers have the chance not just to survive but to develop too. A premium is included in the price for social or environmental projects, or to strengthen their co-operatives. So local communities have the ability to invest in long-term improvement, through elected committees who identify suitable projects. Examples of these include drilling bore-holes for clean water in Malawi, establishing health care centres in Guatemala and providing electricity in Sri Lanka.

Care for the environment is a fundamental tenet of Fairtrade. This means better protection of the interests of the producers as well as better products for the consumer. Organic practices can help protect endangered species (by not using herbicides) and also raise awareness of further ways to protect the environment such as planting, discarding and recycling with care.

Food scares in the UK over recent years are causing us to examine the source and processing of our food in order to safeguard our own health. Fairtrade takes that principle further – to be able to eat and drink for the health and well-being of many previously marginalised people across the world. Buying Fairtrade allows a consistent, steady flow of funds to save others from destitution. Can we put a price on that?

For discussion

Q Is Fairtrade an important issue for you/for others?

Q How much interest have you seen in your locality?

Q What measures can be taken to support it?

Q How easy have you found it to find Fairtrade products in your area?

Q Could you join or start a purchasing scheme to buy in bulk?

Q What are the principles which might make you consider Fairtrade?

Q Has your definition of community changed after reading this section of the book?

Q What changes might you begin to make as a result of some of the stories or ideas you've read?

HAZEL GAYDON

MY RELATIONSHIPS

Relationships

We all have relationships. And these can motivate, excite, fulfil and sustain us more than anything else in this world, particularly when they're going well. We need to take seriously the idea of prioritising relationships, across the whole of our lives.

However, the quality of our days can often be determined by the people we spend time with and this is why all our relationships are important. We often immediately think of the significant other (if there is one) in our lives when we talk of relationships, but the people who serve us in the supermarket or who we sit next to on the bus or work with can have a huge impact on our day.

On a separate sheet of paper make a list of the significant relationships in your life – Partner, children, family, friends, work colleagues, neighbours, acquaintances and others like local shop-keepers, service providers and even pets.

Consider the following questions for each of the people you have listed:

Q How happy are you with this relationship?

Q Are you spending enough quality time with this person?

Q How could you improve this relationship?

We quoted the well known saying of Jesus earlier, 'love your neighbour as yourself' and while most people put the emphasis on the first part of this phrase, the second part is important too. As we learn to love ourselves, respect and believe in who we are and exude a positive self image, then the more these things that we feel on the inside will show on the outside and affect the way others relate to us.

Some life coaching books advise ditching any draining relationships, dropping friendships that don't give us anything positive and only spending time with people who are on our wavelength. While this might sound like an attractive proposition, it's not the way we choose to live. We try to take the words 'love your neighbour as yourself' seriously and so while we do aim to get a balance and give ourselves a bit of pampering now and again, we also feel that a life lived totally for ourselves isn't the route to 'life in all its fullness'.

Having a balanced circle of life isn't about ignoring elderly parents, children with disabilities or challenging behaviour or partners who are suffering from work related or other stresses, but about finding ways of making our current situation work in the best possible way and having a balance between energising, neutral and more difficult relationships.

Make a list of your closest relationships under these three headings.

Energising

Neutral

Difficult relationships

Q How balanced do you think your lists look?

Q What can you do to redress any imbalance?

Coming alongside those who are struggling in various areas of their lives or in those times when our own situations can seem overwhelming can be tough and we both have a card above our desks printed with the words 'This too will pass.'

While it's comforting to know that the hard times won't go on indefinitely, it's also a reminder that those times of extreme happiness and joy will also pass too.

Friendship Groups

Under the title 'Friendship', a recent issue of a popular women's magazine ran an article about groups which are springing up around the country giving 'time poor' women the chance to meet up with others who have similar interests.

The article said 'a minor cultural revolution is taking place as women are joining or forming groups: the structure of prearranged meetings means they get a few hours for themselves, see their friends and join in an activity they enjoy.'

The article then goes on to talk to women involved in a variety of groups under headings like Culture Club, The Knitters, The Gardening Group, The Curry Club and The Good Turn Club, showing how women are using such diverse activities as knitting, allotments and curry evenings as a way of meeting together regularly with a common purpose. It's interesting that activities like knitting and keeping allotments, which only a few years ago were seen as incredibly old-fashioned, are making a huge comeback. Are there hobbies like this which you enjoy that could be developed?

The Curry Club idea could be adapted to a variety of different situations but it was founded when friends struggled to stay in regular contact with each other because of their increasingly busy lives. The group meets monthly in an Indian restaurant and at the end of the meal give it marks out of ten, decide who's had the best meal and compare dishes to those in other restaurants. The group consists of about ten regulars, a mixture of family, friends and work colleagues. 'It's a lot of fun and you get to meet new people.'

New members join the Good Turn Club via the website **www.join-me.co.uk** and make a simple promise to perform a random act of kindness every Friday, either as individuals or as part of a group. The reason behind the group is simple, 'By making someone else feel good, you make yourself feel good too.' We like the way Jesus put it, 'It's better to give than to receive.'

Think of how you could develop ideas like this and build new relationships in your community or workplace.

One idea you could use with a friend or for a girls' night in or out, depending on where you choose to meet, would be to answer the following questions, complied by life coach Bruce Stanley
– www.brucestanley.co.uk

Q Every New Year I resolve to...?

Q I'd be absolutely fantastic at...?

Q Nobody knows I'm...?

Q One thing everyone's tried but me is...?

Q If I wasn't scared I'd...?

Q My dream is to...?

Q If I could change one thing in my life it would be...?

Q I really wish I would no longer...?

Q If money were no object I would...?

Q If success were guaranteed I would...?

Maybe you could take the answers one step further and see what positive steps you could make to ensure that some of the answers become a reality, with the help of friends or family if necessary.

'FRIENDSHIP IS TESTED IN THE THICK YEARS OF SUCCESS, RATHER THAN IN THE THIN YEARS OF STRUGGLE.'
Barry Humphries

'I HAVE LOST FRIENDS, SOME BY DEATH... Virginia Woolf
OTHERS THROUGH SHEER INABILITY TO CROSS THE STREET.'

'I NO DOUBT DESERVED MY ENEMIES, BUT I DON'T BELIEVE I DESERVED MY FRIENDS.'

Walt Whitman

'I CANNOT FORGIVE MY FRIENDS FOR DYING; I DO NOT FIND THESE VANISHING ACTS OF THEIRS AT ALL AMUSING.'

Logan Pearsall Smith

'A FRIEND IS SOMEONE WHO WILL HELP YOU MOVE, Anon

A REAL FRIEND IS SOMEONE WHO WILL HELP YOU MOVE A BODY.'

Marriage

We've both been happily (most of the time!) married for over thirty years each, so come to this area of relationships as fans of the institution, although we have to admit that it's taken lots of hard work and effort to get to the stage we're at now. While neither of us are raging feminists, we believe that a successful marriage is based on team work and allowing each partner to work to their strengths. However, we do love the following story, which illustrates the perception of marriage which was handed to us by our mothers.

Once upon a time, in a land far away, a beautiful, independent, self-assured princess happened upon a frog as she sat, contemplating ecological issues on the shores of an unpolluted pond in a verdant meadow near her castle.

A frog hopped into the princess' lap and said: 'Elegant Lady, I was once a handsome prince, until an evil witch cast a spell upon me. One kiss from you, however and I will turn back into the dapper, young prince that I am and then, my sweet, we can marry and set up housekeeping in your castle with my mother, where you can satisfy my needs, prepare and serve my meals, clean my clothes, bear my children, and forever feel grateful and happy doing so.'

That night, as the princess dined sumptuously on lightly sautéed frog legs seasoned in a white wine and onion cream sauce, she chuckled and thought to herself: I don't think so!

In spite of the dire warning of our message above, some people still dream about a fairytale wedding but don't invest time in maintaining the relationship.

If you're married or in a committed relationship:

Q How do you work at keeping your relationship alive?

Q When could you spend more time together? Can you blank out some time in your diary and stick to it?

Q Do you discuss topical issues and seek each other's opinion?

Q Could you plan a joint project of some sort?

Q Are you able to talk frankly about money, sex, health, friends etc?

Marriage preparation is always a good idea and one of the great benefits of the Personality Profiling tool (PEP™) is that we can offer a couple's comparison report to any two individuals who take the personality profile online.

It's proved to be a helpful and informative tool for couples who can see, almost at a glance, some of the challenges they're likely to face in their future together and gives the opportunity to address them before they cause real issues in the relationship.

Even those who have been married a long time can find the insights helpful. If you think your relationship would benefit from this, log onto **www.in-your-element.co.uk** for more details.

Parent Coaching

Today's parents live hectic lives.

It's the most rewarding and challenging job we'll ever have in our lives but there's so much to fit in and so little time to do it – find their sports kit, make their packed lunch, dress them with matching socks, take them to their next football match, drop them off at their friends, pick them up, buy clothes you don't want them to wear, get their meals ready, make sure they eat the right food, disappear when their friends come round, stop them mixing with the wrong people, tame their tantrums, tidy their bedrooms, talk to them about sex and spend 'quality' time with them. Try to be the perfect parent...

Then, of course, there are all the other things you have to fit in – bills to pay, jobs to do, careers to pursue, housework, shopping, get the car serviced, book the dentist, friends to see, look perfect at all times. The list can be endless, can't it? In fact, it's surprising that we have the energy to do anything at all. Just talking about it all can make us feel exhausted.

Parentalk organise coaching events and workshops at regular intervals during the course of the year and look at a whole variety of different topics from 'Achieving your goals at home and at work' to 'How to make the most of your relationship with your teenager.' Ruth attended a course recently and found it helpful and informative. If you would like details on any of the above, contact Parentalk on: coaching@parentalk.co.uk

There's no such thing as an apprentice parent. It's not something you work your way towards. From the moment the little angel arrives in your life, you begin to lose sleep and it continues until they have left home and sometimes even after that as well.

Many parents will agree that raising children is the hardest yet most fulfilling job they ever do. Years ago it seemed easier when there were accepted parameters beyond which most children didn't go. However today, with more restrictions on parents and more fear of 'doing it wrong', it seems we are breeding a generation of children who are in charge rather than their parents. Never was there more of a need for parents to be empowered in their role. Parenting courses, self-help books and TV programmes abound with advice, yet often we still struggle.

Sometimes parenting can highlight our own inadequacies or bring up issues from the past that we never dealt with. In these cases, some one-to-one sessions with a parent coach will help you work through old hurts and build stronger relationships with your children.

With seven children between us, we believe that the best things we can give our children are roots and wings. There is a great strength to be drawn from solidarity so, if you can get together with other parents as part of a parenting support group and share experiences and insights, it will help to keep every situation in context. Humour is a powerful tool and learning to laugh about things will help to keep you sane.

Q Who is in charge most of the time in your home, parents or children?

Q What are the best things for you about being a parent?

Q What are the hardest?

Q What are the three main areas that need changing?

If the answers to these questions give you cause for concern, then getting together with other parents to discuss some of the issues could be helpful. Ruth asked the parents of her children's friends to help her pilot a parenting group in her home when her older children were young and went on to run groups regularly for several years. They used materials from Family Caring, **www.familycaring.co.uk** who have a number of different courses covering specific age groups, as well as 'Parenting and Sex' and 'Parent Assertiveness' programmes. While the materials are geared towards a group, they could also be helpful to individuals.

The Parent Coaching Academy offers on-line coaching for parents and sends out regular newsletters full of helpful advice. They have developed a seven-day model that motivates parents to tackle family problems with a practical action plan – one day at a time, with the aim of putting mums and dads back in the driving seat. They help parents focus positively on creative solutions to their challenges and develop tailor-made strategies to achieve them, closing the gap between where they are and where they want to be. Their mission is to reduce parents' stress levels and boost their energy, so that they can get the maximum enjoyment from family life. Contact them at www.parentcoachingacademy.co.uk.

If you have children with 'special needs' either because of a specific challenge or due to early trauma, (maybe they have been fostered or adopted) then therapy or specialist help may be needed in finding the best ways to parent these children. Take a look at the Adoption UK website – www.adoptionuk.org and The Fostering Network site – www.fostering.net for details of where to find further help.

Diana Loomans has written a number of books, including 100 ways to build self esteem in your child (HJ Kramer/New World Library, 2003) which gives further inspirational help for parents.

Q So how can you have more fun in your family?

Q What suggestions can you come up with as you exchange ideas with friends and work out ways of really enjoying time with your children?

'PARENTS LEARN A LOT FROM THEIR CHILDREN ABOUT COPING WITH LIFE.'

Muriel Spark

'LIKE ALL THE BEST FAMILIES, WE HAVE OUR SHARE OF ECCENTRICITIES, OF IMPETUOUS AND WAYWARD YOUNGSTERS AND OF FAMILY DISAGREEMENTS.'

Queen Elizabeth II (Daily Mail 1989)

'MOTHER ALWAYS SAID THAT HONESTY WAS THE BEST POLICY AND MONEY WASN'T EVERYTHING. SHE WAS WRONG ABOUT OTHER THINGS TOO.'

Brendan Behan

'MOTHERHOOD IS A DEAD-END JOB. YOU'VE NO SOONER LEARNED THE SKILLS THAN YOU ARE REDUNDANT.'

Claire Rayner

THE HAND THAT ROCKS THE CRADLE IS THE HAND THAT RULES THE WORLD.'

William Ross

Strangers

There is a saying that strangers are friends we've not yet met and some close relationships start with a casual conversation at a social event.

Carole Stone, author of *Networking: The Art of Making More Friends*[24] gives this advice, 'You've just arrived at a party or event – alone. There's no-one there you know. You feel foolish and want to run. Don't.'

- Approach someone else who looks as if they're on their own too. Say, 'I don't seem to know anyone else here. I met Jim/Ann, our host, at a book launch/dinner party. How do you know them?'

- Compliment someone on their appearance or say 'What a beautiful house. Have you been here before?'

- Join in a group by saying 'I hope I'm not butting in but I don't think I know anyone here. Can I introduce myself?'

- If you've finished your drink, turn to someone and say 'I'm just going to get my glass refilled. Can I get you a drink?'

Be aware that relationships happen on different levels and a relationship is still valid even if it's not as close as you would like.

In his book *The Search to Belong*[25], Joseph Myers says that there are four different types of space in which we live out relationships: Public, Social, Personal and Intimate and we probably have significant relationships in all of those areas, most of them being in the public category, with the list getting smaller as we go through the four words.

Public space people may well be those we know in the street, outside school or at work in a large office. Social space is reserved for those we choose to spend time with or go out with for an occasional evening.

Personal space friends are those we share private thoughts with and are able to express ourselves freely with. But the few people we allow into our intimate space are the ones who know the naked truth about us. All the relationships are genuine and significant – just different.

Sex

This may help you understand why it's hard to get close to someone you know, with whom you may even experience feelings of rejection. The chances are that you are trying to draw them into a space that they feel unable to occupy. For reasons of their own, they are still relating to you in a public or social space. So don't feel rejected – simply recognise that your friendship is significant as it is.

Last year we invited our friend, Sheila Bridge, to run a seminar at an Activate conference, on the research she was doing for her new book, *Who Stole Your Sex Life?* (Kingsway, 2007). It was very well attended and had hugely positive feedback. The book has now been published and we would highly recommend it.

Sheila also put us in touch www.whollylove.co.uk – a website full of information and articles about sex within a committed relationship, as well as its own shop. The founders, Stella and Stan, are Christians and received lots of positive publicity as they launched their new site, including the filming of a documentary about them for the BBC.

> **THE SECRET OF LOVE IS SEEKING VARIETY IN YOUR LIFE TOGETHER, AND NEVER LETTING ROUTINE CHORDS DULL THE MELODY OF YOUR ROMANCE.**
>
> **Anonymous**

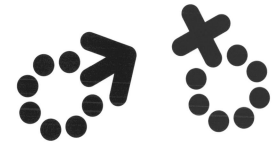

Advice

We think the Bible has some great advice for all sorts of relationships. Here are just a few quotes:

John 13:34[26]

I GIVE YOU A NEW COMMANDMENT, THAT YOU LOVE ONE ANOTHER. JUST AS I HAVE LOVED YOU, YOU ALSO SHOULD LOVE ONE ANOTHER.

A FRIEND IS ALWAYS LOYAL AND A BROTHER IS BORN TO HELP IN TIME OF NEED.

Proverbs 17:17

LOVE IS PATIENT AND KIND.

I Corinthians 13:4

GOD SAID 'IT'S NOT GOOD FOR THE MAN TO BE ALONE.

I'LL MAKE HIM A HELPER, A COMPANION.'

Genesis 2:18 The Message

GOD PLACES THE LONELY IN FAMILIES. Psalm 68:6

CHILDREN ARE A GIFT FROM THE LORD; THEY ARE A REWARD FROM HIM.

Psalm 127:3

Talkback - Supermum

Mother is usually the first person you know and the relationship with her shapes your life. Some people, for whom this relationship was a negative or abusive one, or where the mother wasn't around for various reasons, carry the trauma of this with them throughout their lives. This is not just for childhood; it is for ever.

For most people, however, her approval helps to build confidence in childhood and continues to matter long after we have grown up. Her listening to us, her understanding, her interest in our affairs, all confirm the bond of affection between us.

In their book[27] *How to Manage your Mother*, psychotherapist Alyce Faye Cleese and Brian Bates share their concerns. It appears that smooth transitions in relating – from being a child through to a more mature communication with a mother – are very rare. Criticism, interfering, complaining and continuing to treat as children were the most often used words about the experience. Many mothers do not find it easy to praise.

Seemingly small incidents with one's mother can remain as memories for life. The following are all real-life quotes from conversations Jan has had in the recent past.

'I dreaded her standing there expecting a kiss – I was frightened of her. She had to cope with seven of us after my father was killed and she thought hard discipline was the only way.'

'You see they really wanted a son; so I could never change their disappointment. I threw myself into school work and excelled in a way I never could at home.'

'It was after a school parents' evening. She stood in my bedroom doorway and said: I was ashamed to be your mother tonight.'

'It was obvious I was her favourite. Apart from the potential for resentment by the others, it put enormous pressure on me to reach her high standards.'

But it's not plain sailing for mothers either.

'I get so annoyed when my son's wife says she'll get him to call me. He either phones because he chooses to or I'd rather he didn't phone at all.'

'I don't like to interfere. I once suggested they might leave him to cry and she said the baby book said that was cruel.'

'It's easy to think you've failed. They grow up, get involved with demanding jobs and making money, but relationships don't seem a priority.'

'If I don't give in she sulks and tells me her friends' mothers are much nicer than me.'

So what are we to do? Do mothers or children have any chance of growing up and growing older in a happy way? Maybe the answer, though hard to attain all the time, lies in these words

Love is patient, love is kind. It does not envy, it does not boast, it is not proud. It is not rude, it is not self-seeking, it is not easily angered, it keeps no record of wrongs. Love does not delight in evil but rejoices with the truth. It always protects, always trusts, always hopes, always perseveres. 1 Corinthians 13:4-6.

For discussion

Q What was the best lesson you learnt from your own mother?

Q What is the hardest challenge for mothers today?

Q How could mothers best be supported by those around them?

Q Is there a way you could make life easier for a mother you know?

Q Have you found the Corinthians recipe helpful in your experience?

Q How often have you managed to live it out?

Q What was the secret?

HAZEL GAYDON

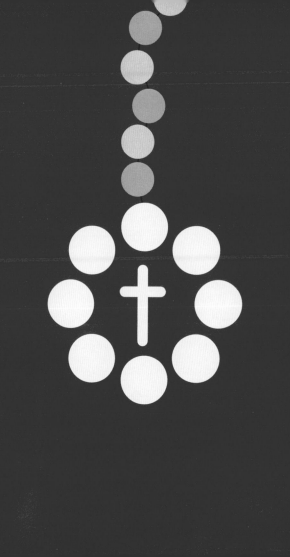

MY FAITH JOURNEY

Spirituality

Spirituality: The state or quality of being dedicated to God, religion or spiritual things or values, especially as contrasted with material or temporal ones.

We've included this section on spirituality in our life circle as we believe that most of us are looking for something to fulfil that aspect of our lives, though we might choose to look for the answer in different places.

In the 21st century we live in a spiritual-supermarket culture. So there are lots of places that claim to have the answers and a mass of resources for spiritual searchers to explore.

Change is all around us, especially in technology and the world of information, but also in the way we live. Our lives have had to speed up in order to cope with the many things we try to juggle. Little wonder that people are beginning to recognise that they must take some time out in order to de-stress.

For some, the gentle pace of the institutionalized religions can be attractive and they are deliberately opting out of the rat race – if only for the weekend. Recent television documentaries like 'The Monastery' and 'The Convent' – where people joined in the gentle rhythm of a religious community – have raised the profile of retreats. If you're interested in this, log onto The Retreat Association website – **www.retreats.org.uk**

For some people 'time out' will simply be time to relax and take up a relaxing hobby, but for many a retreat provides the opportunity to explore faith issues and possibly to look afresh at a faith they professed many years ago before work, study and family life crowded in.

It's universally accepted that some quiet space in each day, away from the pressures of life, to reflect and be still, is valuable. Some would say it is essential to a balanced life.

Q Do you take time out to meditate?

Q If so, what works best for you?

One of our friends, Kate Austin, is an artist who has produced a set of DVDs which have been created to help us be still in our busy lives. They each consist of fifteen minutes of beautiful and inspiring artwork set to gentle music, designed to take the viewer on a contemplative journey – **www.christart.co.uk**. We recommend them as a great place to start.

Conversely, a growing number of people have chosen a simpler lifestyle yet, at the moment, do not equate this with a faith journey. But that doesn't mean they have ruled it out for ever. Whilst they might discount the Church as having any real relevance, for many the person of Jesus still holds an attraction. The comedian Billy Connolly is quoted as saying 'I can't believe in Christianity but I think Jesus was a wonderful man.'

As we, the authors are both Christians, we too think Jesus was a wonderful man and we draw heavily on his life and teaching for our inspiration. Whether you believe he is who he claimed to be (the Son of God), or consider him a prophet, or simply an all round good guy who features in history, there is no doubt that Jesus was a charismatic character who drew the crowds.

Many claimed to be healed through his ministry and all who followed and listened to him found his words to be powerful and life-changing. He was also a dab hand at the art of prayer.

Prayer

That question, 'How do we pray?' is still asked today of religious leaders. Here is a great explanation offered recently by Archbishop Rowan Williams for 'Pause for Thought' on Radio 2.

'I don't know how well placed I am, but what I do know is that many people find difficulty with prayer... it's one thing to talk about it but quite another to do it... and one of the questions I've often been asked is 'Have you any tips on how to pray?'

Let me put it this way. I'm not much of a one for sunbathing; too much lying around and I get fidgety and a bit guilty. But there's something about sunbathing that tells us more about what prayer is like than any amount of religious jargon.

When you're lying on the beach or under the lamp, something is happening, something that has nothing to do with how you feel or how hard you're trying. You're not going to get a better tan by screwing up your eyes and concentrating. You give the time and that's it. All you have to do is turn up. And then things change at their own pace. You simply have to be there where the light can get at you.

People often have the impression that praying is anxiously putting on your best clothes, finding acceptable things to say in the right sort of language, generally getting your act together – oh and concentrating, of course. But when in the Bible Jesus advises his friends about how to pray, he tells them not to worry about any of this. Say, 'Father', he tells them. Just be confident that you're welcome as you would be at home. All you need to do is to be where the light can get at you – in this case, the light of God's love.

Give the time and let go of trying hard (actually this is the difficult bit). God is there always. You don't need to fight for his attention or make yourself acceptable. He's glad to see you. And he'll make a difference while you're not watching, just by radiating who and what he is in your direction. All he asks is that you stay there with him for a bit, in the light. For the rest, you just trust him to get on with it.'

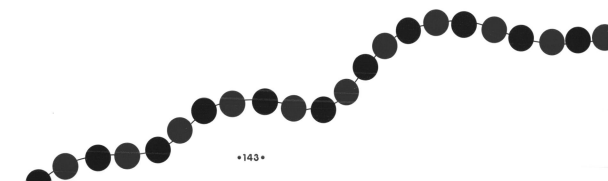

Rewriting the Rules

Sin is out of fashion – that is the conclusion arrived at by 'The Heaven and Earth Show'.

The Sunday morning BBC1 programme commissioned a survey of 1001 adults and 9 per cent of the respondents said that they had never committed any of the 'seven deadly sins' as listed by Thomas Aquinas in the thirteenth century – pride, envy, anger, sloth, greed, gluttony, lust. (The Bible gives the original list in chapter 6 of the book of Proverbs.)

Some believe that the list is culturally driven and could do with an update. So we include the new list for your edification: cruelty, adultery, bigotry, dishonesty, hypocrisy, greed and selfishness.

Channel 4 decided that the Ten Commandments could do with a facelift and a TV programme was recently devoted to discussing them.

With God's Ten Commandments, Moses outlined a basis for life and morality which has lasted 3,500 years and been embraced by Christians, Jews and Muslims alike. Channel 4 decided to find out whether the British public thought the Ten Commandments were still relevant today and commissioned a national survey. Forty thousand people voted and the top twenty suggestions formed the basis of a special programme during which some of Britain's familiar figures from celebrities to religious leaders debated the list.

Seven of the original commandments went out in the new poll but were replaced with others largely based on biblical principles. 'Be true to yourself' was the only exception to this.

'CANDIDATES SHOULD NOT ATTEMPT MORE THAN SIX OF THESE.'

Hilaire Beloc
(1870-1953. Liberal MP, writer and critic)

The top twenty new Commandments were:

20 Be honest

19 Don't kill

18 Respect your mother and father

17 Enjoy life

16 Nothing in excess

15 Be true to your own God

14 Treat others as you would like to be treated

13 Protect your family

12 Try your best at all times

11 Look after your health

10 Don't commit adultery

9 Live within your means

8 Appreciate what you have

7 Never be violent

6 Protect the environment

5 Protect and nurture children

4 Take responsibility for your own actions

3 Don't steal

2 Be true to yourself

The winning commandment was

1 'Treat others as you would like to be treated.'

Q Consider the list opposite and what it says about our society today. How far removed do you think these new commandments are from the original ten in the Bible? These can be found in the second book which is Exodus Chapter 20.

Things go round in circles and it seems that the lifestyle which more and more people are now aspiring to is the one that was actually intended for us in the first place. So let's go right back to the beginning of time as we know it and look at the original plan...

Natural Woman

In the beginning God made... woman. That was after he'd got in some practice beforehand with man...

But the truth is that when God put you together, he was working to a blueprint that was unique. He designed you 'after his own image', yet as an individual with a personality. His plan was for you to be happy in your own skin, going with the grain of who you are and feeling complete.

He intended you to have a perfect relationship with him, to spend time talking and listening and enjoying his company. He gave you a brain so that you could debate and challenge, taking an interest in global events and having a point of view. He saw your potential and hoped that you'd explore it and feel fulfilled.

He expected that you'd enjoy the wonders of creation, caring for 'the Garden', where good organic food grew, including ingredients for every beauty product you could ever want (and for every cleaning product you would ever feel obliged to use) and for you to feel healthy.

As you're a 'chip off the old block' he assumed you'd be creative, enjoying making beautiful or useful things, appreciating colours and pictures, releasing the music he planted in your heart by singing. And, naturally, you've inherited his sense of humour (haven't you?). He wanted you to follow his lead and take time off, resting, enjoying leisure pursuits and getting the right amount of sleep. His desire was for you to live in harmony with others, reflecting his love to those around you.

We can't help thinking that it does sound like an attractive deal. So it would seem to us that if there was a way of squeezing ourselves back into the original mould we should go for it. The squeezing bit might be trickier for some than others – there is no mention of sticky toffee pudding in Eden and the Atkins diet was out of the question!

Maybe this is your time to consider what God means in your life. Have you ever thought about it? What about Jesus? There have been so many films made about various aspects of his life that you might even have a picture in your head of how he looks. Most of the films we've seen depict him as an incredibly attractive person. Why not try watching a film or reading through one of the Gospels (the first four books in the New Testament, Matthew, Mark, Luke and John) and see what they say about Jesus. Look at the rejesus website too, **www.rejesus.co.uk**

Talkback - Spiritual Journey

Spirituality and health are closely linked. Tapping those two words into a search engine on the internet brings up an overwhelming response.

Though the different sources might want to look at spirituality in different ways, all acknowledge the idea that we are spiritual beings, that spirituality brings a sense of peace and wholeness which is beneficial to health and that we function better in every way when we are aware of our spiritual needs and tend to them, just as we look after our bodies in a practical way with water, food, exercise and fresh air.

Professionals who are caring for older people have recognised that those with a faith tend to be more optimistic generally and less fearful about death and illness. This may be related to the idea that Somebody, somewhere is in control of the universe and for many of our older generation, that someone is the God of the Bible.

When our grandparents were growing up, churchgoing was the norm on a Sunday, with many families attending several times during the day.

Bible stories were taught in school and school assemblies were held, which included worship as well as a strong moral message with biblical roots.

As culture has changed and churchgoing has dwindled, there are many families who have no real understanding of the Christian message and won't therefore have that deeply rooted belief system to draw upon in a crisis, in their old age or simply even to enrich their lives on a daily basis. They don't know themselves to be loved and accepted unconditionally and it shows.

Sometimes, through well-meaning but ill-advised individuals, people can be given a rather one-sided version of God as avenging, angry and judgemental Father, or bowed and defeated on the cross – Jesus, who appeared to lose the fight against good and evil. For others an unhealthy interest in the occult creates a feeling of darkness and helplessness.

For Discussion

Q What has your own spiritual journey been like?

Q Did you attend church as a child or in later life?

Q If so what drew you to go there
– did you have a choice?

Q What image of God was drawn for you by this experience?

Q Was this an image that was drawn for you by someone else?

Q Did you read anything from the Bible or do you read it now?

Q Do you ever pray? If so, who to?

Q Do you feel that anyone is listening or that your prayers are answered?

Q Does prayer make you feel better?

Q Have you ever said 'Thank you' to God for good things or beauty that you see around you?

Q If not, would you be willing to give it a try?

There are a variety of courses available to explore faith and they are all aimed at different people. For example, the Essence course[28] was written for spiritual searchers who have a particular interest in New Age philiosophies. The Start course[29] is actually a really good place to start and is filmed at a seaside resort. Other courses, like the well-advertised Alpha course[30], are useful as a moving on stage for those who have decided that they are interested in Christianity and want to know more. A walk around a Christian bookshop will illuminate how much material is available.

This is your journey to make and, as we said earlier in the book, no-one can make this for you but we are both Christians and happy to recommend this as a way of life. Jesus said he had come so that we might have life in all its fullness and that's what we set out to explore in writing this book – so this has been our journey as well as yours.

Q What might fullness of life mean for you?

Church is not the only way to explore this – small discussion groups and Bible study groups are a good way to explore and even deepen faith. We both work for Activate, which exists to Activate your mind, your faith, your life. We would love to think that we have achieved this and wherever you are on your spiritual journey that this book might have moved you on a step.

Check us out at www.activateyourlife.org.uk

Full circle

Q Now go back to our circle and plot your graph again. Have any of your markers moved?

We would love to think that your circle is now looking a better shape and that you are on the way to finding life in all its fullness. If you need some help in any of those areas, why not contact us via our website www.in-your-element.co.uk

To finish this section why not take a look at www.fathersloveletter.com? It's a collection of different verses put together in the form of a letter – the video version is well worth a look.

We hope you've found our book informative, refreshing, inspirational and fun.

If you enjoyed reading it and want to have more of our resources you can find them on the Activate website www.activateyourlife.org.uk

If you would like to be part of a nationwide team of people who enjoy being who they are and using those gifts and talents to share God's love in the community, we'd love to have you with us.

Ruth & Jan

'WE MUST RESPECT THE OTHER FELLOW'S RELIGION, BUT ONLY IN THE SENSE AND TO THE EXTENT THAT WE RESPECT HIS THEORY THAT HIS WIFE IS BEAUTIFUL AND HIS CHILDREN SMART.'

H.L. MENCKEN

'TO BELIEVE ONLY POSSIBILITIES IS NOT FAITH BUT MERE PHILOSOPHY.'

Sir Thomas Browne

'A FAITH IS SOMETHING YOU DIE FOR; A DOCTRINE IS SOMETHING YOU KILL FOR; THERE IS ALL THE DIFFERENCE IN THE WORLD.'

Tony Benn

'A SINGLE GRATEFUL THOUGHT RAISED TO HEAVEN IS THE MOST PERFECT PRAYER.'

Gotthold Ephraim Lessing

NOTHING IS MORE PRACTICAL THAN FINDING GOD, THAT IS, THAN FALLING IN LOVE IN A QUITE ABSOLUTE FINAL WAY. WHAT YOU ARE IN LOVE WITH, WHAT SEIZES YOUR IMAGINATION, WILL AFFECT EVERYTHING.

IT WILL DECIDE WHAT WILL GET YOU OUT OF BED IN THE MORNING, WHAT YOU DO WITH YOUR EVENINGS, HOW YOU SPEND YOUR WEEKENDS, WHAT YOU READ, WHO YOU KNOW, WHAT BREAKS YOUR HEART AND WHAT AMAZES YOU WITH JOY AND GRATITUDE. FALL IN LOVE, STAY IN LOVE AND IT WILL DECIDE EVERYTHING.

Pedro Arrupe SJ

Appendix

1   Laurie Beth Jones, *The Four Elements of Success* (Nashville: Nelson publishers, 2005)

2   Laurie Beth Jones, *The Path* (New York: Hyperion books,1996)

3   Judith Holder, *Grumpy Old Women* (London: BBC Books, 2006)

4   Oliver James, *Affluenza - how to be successful and stay sane* (London: Vermilion books, 2007)

5   *The Climate Movement, I count – your step-by-step guide to climate bliss* (London: Penguin, 2006)

6   Copyright BBC – used with permission – www.bbc.co.uk/religion

7   Po Bronson, *What should I do With My Life?* (Random House, 2003)

8   www.pobronson.com

9   Steve Chalke and John Byrne, *How to Succeed as a Working Parent* (London: Hodder & Stoughton, 2003)

10 Carl Honoré, *In Praise of Slow – how a worldwide movement is challenging the culture of speed* (London: Orion, 2005)

11 www.inpraiseofslow.com

12 http://www.rivercottage.net/index.jsp

13 www.downshiftingweek.com

14 5th November 2006

15 Phil Isherwood, *Life Behind the Petunias* (Towpath Press 1999)

16 Sarah Stacey and Jo Fairley, *The 21st Century Beauty Bible* (London: Kyle Cathie, 2002)

17 Jo Fairley, *The Ultimate Natural Beauty Book* (London: Kyle Cathie, 2004)

18 Janey Lee Grace, *Imperfectly Natural Woman* (Carmathen: Crown House publishing, 2006)

19 *The Week* 26/8/06

20 R Adams & J Harney, *Unlocking the Door* (Milton Keynes: Authentic media, 2005)

21   *Change the World for a Fiver*
     (London: Short Books, 2004)

22   *Change the World 9-5: 50 ways to change the world at work* (London: Short Books, 2007)

23   Duncan Clark, *The Rough Guide to Ethical Shopping* (London: Rough Guides Ltd, 2004)

24   Carole Stone, *Networking – the art of making more friends* (London: Vermilion, 2001)

25   Joseph Myers, *The Search to Belong* (Grand Rapids: Zondervan, 2003)

26   New Revised Standard Version

27   Alyce Faye Cleese and Brian Bates, *How to Manage Your Mother* (London: Arrow books, 2003)

28   For more information, go to www.sharejesusinternational.com

29   For more information, go to www.stps.org.uk

30   For more information, go to www.alpha.org

Notes

Notes

Notes

Freewheeling

How to let go a little, love a lot and discover life in all its fullness